PLANNED PUBLIC RELATIONS FOR LIBRARIES

a PPRG handbook

edited by Margaret Kinnell

Published on behalf of the
Publicity and Public Relations Group (PPRG)
of the Library Association
by

TAYLOR GRAHAM

© Taylor Graham and contributors 1989

Published by
Taylor Graham
500 Chesham House
150 Regent St
LONDON W1R 5FA
United Kingdom

Taylor Graham
Suite 187
12021 Wilshire Boulevard
LOS ANGELES
CA 90025
USA

ISBN 0 947568 31 X

Printed by Information Press Ltd., Oxford, England.

CONTENTS

Foreword
JOHN B. LAVELLE   1

Introduction
MARGARET KINNELL   3

Public relations: the commercial approach
JON WHITE   9

User needs
COLIN HARRIS   17

Planning a campaign: public libraries
JOE HENDRY   25

Planning a campaign: the special library and information service
SYLVIA P. WEBB   36

Budgeting and costing campaign activities: paying the price and value for money
STEPHEN A. ROBERTS   46

Political lobbying
GEORGE CUNNINGHAM   59

Educating staff for public relations
DARLENE E. WEINGAND   68

Training and educating staff for public relations
JON PYLE   78

Evaluating a campaign programme
DAVID PICKTON   88

The importance of public relations in information service organizations
BOB USHERWOOD   110

FOREWORD

No association or business, however exclusive, can exist in isolation. Bridges must be built to establish optimum public response. A good public relations policy recognises that there is an obligation to publics beyond those with which it is directly concerned, indeed to society as a whole.

The Institute of Public Relations, the professional body representing 2,600 individual PR practitioners, defines Public Relations as the planned and sustained effort to establish and maintain goodwill and mutual understanding between an organisation and its publics.

Two recent category winners in the much coveted Sword of Excellence Awards have achieved their objectives on a budget of less than £5,000 — an effective PR campaign can benefit *every* organisation, irrespective of size.

John B. Lavelle
Executive Director,
The Institute of Public Relations

INTRODUCTION
Margaret Kinnell

There is general agreement in the library and information sectors on the importance of a planned approach to marketing services. We have seen a veritable revolution in the thinking on this in recent years. And yet the literature on the subject is sparse on how to set about a key aspect of relating effectively to the market — through well-judged public relations.

This book, commissioned by the Publicity and Public Relations Group of the Library Association, aims to meet the need for such a guide to the planning and implementation of PR in libraries and information services. The authors have de-mystified what to some has seemed the preserve of slick advertising techniques and provided a handbook to good PR practice in the library. Professionalism in librarianship now demands that library managers exploit business techniques for all they are worth. For only in that way can we ensure libraries remain in the forefront of the information society. We can also learn from the experience of successful, PR conscious librarians — marketing techniques *must* meet the needs of librarians and their users if they are really to serve as useful library management tools. Good practice should be disseminated as widely as possible to ensure this happens. This is stating the obvious, but it is only too easy for marketing ideology to take over: librarians have decreasing time to undertake a seemingly ever-increasing workload — and with dwindling resources. Marketing principles need to be informed by relevant professional activities: PR is an essential means of achieving objectives, but it must be practicable. The authors of this Handbook have recognised these sometimes conflicting twin demands: a thoroughly professional approach to library PR that applies the relevant aspects of business practice to the service sector, together with examples of 'how to', within realistic resource limitations.

In Chapter One, the commercial approach to public relations is considered by **Dr. Jon White**, Director of the Executive MBA Programme in Public Relations at the Cranfield School of Management and Director of External Affairs for the School. He is an accredited public relations practitioner with experience in government public affairs with a Canadian provincial government and as a consultant with public and private sector organisations in Canada and the United Kingdom. Before taking up his position at

Cranfield in 1986, he was Chairman of the Academic Department of Public Relations at Mount Saint Vincent University in Canada, which offers a four-year degree programme in public relations. He has a long-standing interest in training for public relations practice and has carried out studies of practitioners' professional development needs in the UK, Canada and the United States. He holds a doctorate in Psychology from the University of London.

In Chapter Two, **Colin Harris** considers the needs of users and how these may be assessed by librarians before planning a campaign. Since 1984 he has been University Librarian at Salford University and is also now their Director of Academic Information Services. Before going to Salford he was a researcher at Newcastle Polytechnic in user studies, working particularly on the Travelling Workshops Experiment, and then in 1979 became Director of the Centre for Research on User Studies at the University of Sheffield until his appointment at Salford in 1984.

A graduate of Hull University, McMaster University, the University of Western Ontario, and recently the Open University, he was awarded the Fellowship of the Library Association in 1986, and is the founding editor of the *British Journal of Academic Librarianship*.

Chapter Three, which looks at planning a campaign from the public librarian's viewpoint is written by **Joe Hendry**, Chief Librarian of Renfrew Libraries Service. He began service in the Mitchell Library in 1963 as a Trainee Librarian and attended library school at the University of Strathclyde from 1964-66, then qualifying as an Associate of the Library Association. In 1972 he was awarded the Fellowship of the Library Association and in 1974 his book *A social history of branch library development* was published by the Scottish Library Association. In 1978 he completed a post-graduate thesis on Septimus Pitt, the most outstanding British Librarian between the two World Wars, and is at present researching a Ph.D. on the role of the public library service in serving the disadvantaged in British society. In 1972 he left his post as Chief Assistant in the Mitchell Library to become Depute Burgh Librarian of Greenock and in 1974 was appointed Chief Librarian for Renfrew District Council; at 29 years of age he was at that time the youngest Chief Librarian in the United Kingdom.

In Chapter Four, **Sylvia Webb,** until recently Head of Business Information at Stoy Hayward, looks at planning a campaign in the special library. She has worked in a variety of information environments, from public libraries to industry, including a number of years as College Librarian at Ashridge Management College. While working at Ashridge, she also lectured in the behavioural sciences, particularly in the areas of motivation, group behaviour, inter-personal skills and communication. She has since been responsible for the design and implementation of several new courses on various aspects of training and information management.

She is currently Manager, Information and Research Services of MSL International (UK) Ltd., is an active member of the Library Association Council, and chairs their Special Libraries Panel. Amongst her contributions to the literature on library management is *Personal development in information work* (Aslib, 1986), which aimed to define personal development in the context of information work whilst not losing sight of the need to view it in a wider organisational context.

Chapter Five, which looks at the financial management of campaign programmes through budgeting and costing, is written by **Dr. Stephen Roberts,** Senior Lecturer in the Department of Information Studies and Technology at Ealing College of Higher Education in London. His teaching interests cover organisation and management studies, access to information, and information and communication in the social sciences and related areas. He is the author of *Cost management for library and information services* (Butterworths, 1985) and editor of *Costing and the economics of library and information services (*Aslib Reader Series, 1984), and as such has an interest in the varied economic and financial issues related to library and information services and the information economy. He was a member of research project teams at the universities of Bath, Cambridge and Loughborough. Current professional activities involve work with IFLA (Section on Library Theory and Research) and the European Committee for Social Science Information and Documentation (ECSSID), continuing education, staffing studies, professional communication, investigation and research in information studies, and educational links with China.

In Chapter Six, **George Cunningham,** Chief Executive of the Library Association since 1984, describes how to lobby politicians successfully. He began his career in the world of diplomacy, serving in the Commonwealth Relations Office in Whitehall and in the British High Commission in Canada. In 1963 he quit government service to enter active politics as an official of the Labour Party. He returned to Whitehall for a couple of years before he was elected as Member of Parliament for Islington South in 1970, representing that constituency for thirteen years, first for Labour and later for the SDP. From 1978 to 1979 he was also a member of the European Parliament. He has written two books: *The management of aid agencies* (1974) and *Careers in politics* (1984). He was also the editor of *Britain and the world in the seventies,* a collection of essays on international affairs (1970).

Chapter Seven, written by **Dr. Darlene E. Weingand,** looks at the education programmes needed to equip professional librarians with the skills and knowledge to embark on campaign programmes. She is Associate Professor at the University of Wisconsin-Madison School of Library and Information Studies and also the Director of the School's Continuing

Education Services. She received her Ph.D. in Adult Education and Library Science at the University of Minnesota in 1980 and her Master of Arts in Library Science from Rosary College in 1973. For eight years, she served as Community Librarian at the Minneapolis Public Library and Information Center. She is the author of several books and numerous journal articles, including *Marketing/planning library and information services* (Libraries Unlimited, 1987) and *The organic public library (*Libraries Unlimited, 1984. Professor Weingand has just recently completed a term as Fulbright Professor at the University of Iceland in Spring 1988.

Chapter Eight, by **Jon Pyle,** considers how staff development and training can aid effective PR campaigning. He holds higher degrees from Manchester and Sheffield Universities and is an Associate of the Library Association. One of 'a very rare breed', he is a publicity manager in a UK public library. As Publications Officer with Sheffield City Libraries since 1980, he has been responsible for publicity, for the library's publishing programme and for the Central Library shop — with the aid of an assistant, a graphic designer and a shop manager. He first suggested the creation of the Publicity and Public Relations Group, was its first chairperson from 1984 to 1987, and now edits *Public Eye,* the PPRG newsletter, and is one of the panel of judges for the Library Association/T.C. Farries Public Relations and Publicity Awards.

In Chapter Nine, **David W. Pickton,** Principal Lecturer at Leicester Polytechnic and Head of their marketing group, describes how to evaluate a campaign programme. He is a qualified, professional member of the Institute of Marketing, the Communications, Advertising and Marketing Society and the British Institute of Management and holds an M.A. in Marketing Management from Lancaster University. He has worked in industry and the public sector in marketing and advertising positions, and is at present an Open University consultant, an Institute of Marketing assistant examiner, Marketing Education Group Regional Chairman, and Director of Isham Management Associates Ltd. He undertakes research and consultancy within the private and public sector and has run courses for and given talks to numerous organisations, including the Publicity and Public Relations Group of the Library Association and the Association of Assistant Librarians, on various marketing topics.

In Chapter Ten, the concluding chapter, **Bob Usherwood,** Senior Lecturer in Librarianship at Sheffield University's Department of Information Studies, assesses the significance of PR in library and information services. He has over fourteen years experience in library education and has had senior management experience in several public library services. Immediately prior to his appointment at Sheffield he was Chief Librarian in the London Borough of Lambeth. In 1976 he was invited by the then Minister for the Arts to join the Library Advisory Council, and he also served on the Library Association Council and chaired a number of its committees including that concerned with professional ethics. In 1978 he received the Senior Librarian's Award, which enabled him to investigate library PR and marketing activities in the United States. Partly as a result of this investigation he wrote *The visible library;* he is the author of numerous other publications and has lectured widely in this country and overseas.

CHAPTER ONE
PUBLIC RELATIONS — THE COMMERCIAL APPROACH
Jon White

Public relations is an important part of the management of the modern business organisation. It is also an important part of the management of other kinds of organisations, such as hospitals, universities, charitable groups and public service organisations, but this chapter is going to focus on lessons that can be drawn from commercial approaches to public relations.

The public relations 'industry', made up of practitioners working in public relations consultancies and in 'in-house' public relations units within organisations, has been growing rapidly in the United Kingdom over the last few years. The trade publication, *PR Week,* has pointed to a growth rate in the industry in cash terms of between 20% to 40% each year in recent years.

Growth in the industry and in the importance of public relations in management are accounted for by the increased competition — national and international — faced by commercial organisations and by the changed expectations the general public have of all organisations. These are summarised in an article which appeared in *Business Week* magazine in January, 1979.[1] According to this article, the modern business organisation is confronted by a more demanding and critical public who can readily turn to competitors if demands for satisfactory services and products are not met.

Competition is now global; British consumer goods companies, for example, now have to contend with competition from companies based around the Pacific Rim, in countries like Japan and Korea, as well as with longer standing competition from the United States and West Germany. The general public and government also look to private sector organisations as sources of funding for community initiatives, and as employers who have an obvious contribution to make to the problems of unemployment, as well as to the solution of other social problems.

Much more than in the past, the managers of business organisations have to take the concerns of groups outside the organisation — consumers, governments and the news media, for example — into account in their decision making and actions. They also have to give more consideration to relations with their own work forces. Employees are now generally better educated than in the past and, even against a background of high levels of unemployment, have raised expectations regarding the rewards they derive from their employment. These rewards are no longer solely monetary: employees hope for certain levels of satisfaction from their employment, and expect to be treated with consideration in their relations with their employers.

Public relations as a practice has developed in response to pressures on organisations. In the United States, it developed as a corporate response to criticisms from the press, which focused on business malpractices. In the United Kingdom, the recent growth of practice is a response to competitive, government and consumer pressures on business organisations.

But what exactly is the contribution of public relations to the management of a business organisation? Put into its most simple and practical terms, public relations is the part of the overall management task which concerns itself with the management of key relationships between business organisations and their publics. Publics include internal groups, such as employees and shareholders, and external groups such as consumers, government, the media, the local communities in which company offices and facilities are located, potential employees, suppliers and so on. Management of key relationships involves identifying their current state and setting objectives for their future development. It also involves anticipating sources of disruption to important relationships and identifying the interests of groups who are parties to key relationships, so that they can be reconciled.

In public relations practice, communication is used in an attempt to influence, sustain or change important relationships, but the desired effects from public relations activities are changes in behaviour. These changes in behaviour can be expressed in increased political support, more consumer demand for products or services, or perhaps a lessening of vocal opposition to a company's expansion. In practice, public relations represents an organisation to its publics, taking into account their interests, with the intention of winning support for, or at least minimising opposition to, an organisation's intentions and activities.

Public relations practice also has an important contribution to make within organisations. In addition to work directed at external publics, public relations in practice may also include efforts to change the behaviour of the organisation on whose behalf it is practised. These internal efforts will be required when, for example, comments from external publics indicate that they find the organisation's performance unsatisfactory; when the organisation wishes to make claims about its performance which cannot be properly made unless performance has improved, or when the public relations practitioner perceives that some organisation intentions or activities run counter to the public interest.

THE COMMERCIAL APPROACH

Let us look at an example to illustrate these points about public relations practice. The Autumn 1987 issue of the Institute of Public Relations journal[2] contains summaries of award winning public relations campaigns. One of these refers to a campaign undertaken by the Tobacco Alliance to defend its members against the consequence of tobacco tax increases. The Tobacco Alliance is a communications network for tobacco companies and their allies. It was set up in 1983 as an off-shoot of the Tobacco Advisory Council, the manufacturing industries' trade association. Its aim is to bring together people whose livelihood depends on tobacco and one of its continuing objectives has been to win fair treatment on tobacco taxes. As an organisation, it is built on relationships between sponsoring companies and allies. It has important relationships with government, the media, industry supporters such as tobacco retailers and opponents such as interest groups concerned to combat the effects of smoking on health. These relationships have to be managed, to continue the co-ordinated effort of industry groups to defend themselves against threats to the industry's interests and to minimise opposition to the industry's legitimate activities.

The case study describes one crucial relationship and the approach taken to managing it by the Alliance. As the journal article points out, any public affairs programme designed by the Alliance to affect a forthcoming budget has a target audience of ultimately only one person: the Chancellor of the Exchequer. In order to influence the Chancellor, other relationships have to be managed. These include political and media groups and parliamentary critics who would have to be convinced that a tax freeze on tobacco products was necessary. Tobacco retailers, as a group, were enlisted in the 1987 campaign to put the tobacco industries' case to members of parliament, for them to transmit the industries' message onwards to government.

The arguments against tobacco tax rises were also distilled and reproduced in a video and booklet designed for viewing and reading by members of parliament. Two hundred and fifty members of parliament were targeted, selected because of constituency tobacco interests, ministerial or opposition rank, house or party committee office or small electoral majorities. Successful presentation of the Alliance case depended on meticulous co-ordination of activity and timing — a detailed schedule incorporated in an action manual specified when Alliance representatives would contact MPs and a mass lobby at Westminster supplemented the individual contacts made.

The public relations consultancy working with the Alliance judged the public relations programme a success in meeting its main objectives. In the event, extra tax on tobacco products was not levied. The Alliance objectives of putting and winning support for the tobacco industry's case were achieved: the arguments against increasing tax reached many parliamentarians by way of third parties. Considerable and sympathetic media coverage of the tobacco industry's case was also generated.

Another recent example of the importance of public relations to the modern business organisation is provided by the Eurotunnel project. This massive project has had, and will probably continue to have for some years, problems of credibility. A number of organisations and groups in the United Kingdom either do not want the project to go ahead or believe that the project is unlikely to be brought to a satisfactory conclusion. The consortium which is to build the tunnel has had to work against its opponents and those groups who doubt the project's viability. This work was especially important during 1987, at a time when the consortium had been looking to investors to support the project. Public relations activities were directed at refuting the arguments put forwad by the project's detractors, building the credibility of the project, convincing the investing public that an investment in Eurotunnel would be likely to be worthwhile, and creating awareness of the project's potential benefits for UK and European economic development.

Despite large-scale falls in share prices in New York, London and Tokyo in the latter part of 1987, the Eurotunnel share offering in the November of 1987 was, although not fully supported by investors, well subscribed. The project itself, despite its detractors and the problems which are bound to affect a large and international construction project, is now more credible and supported by significant groups such as investors, national and local politicians. Specific public relations activities undertaken to support the Eurotunnel project have included briefings of important groups, extensive media relations work and national and regional exhibitions (including a special train which toured the United Kingdom to provide a travelling exhibit). In preparation for the share offering, large investments were made in newspaper and television advertising.

It is clear in these two examples how public relations practice is implemented. In routine cases, public relations activities are undertaken by business organisations to win understanding and support, to maintain their credibility and reputation and to minimise opposition. We need to look briefly now at how public relations activities are managed.

Commercial organisations make one of a number of choices regarding the management of public relations activities carried out on their behalf. As a task of management, public relations can be retained as a responsibility of senior management, or delegated to an external consultancy or to an in-house department of public relations (or some combination of in-house department and external consultancy). Whichever of these options is chosen will depend on the organisation's assessment of its own needs and its understanding of the scope of public relations. For example, an organisation whose senior management believes that the organisation's needs are for a defensive programme of media relations may choose to work with an external consultancy whose brief will extend only to working with the media on the organisation's behalf. Another organisation, working

THE COMMERCIAL APPROACH

from a broader conception of public relations, may establish and maintain a fully staffed department which will manage government relations, public affairs and corporate responsibility programmes, media and investor relations, corporate identity and internal communications programmes.

To emphasize, whichever option is chosen will depend on an accurate assessment of the organisation's needs and a complete understanding of the scope of public relations and the contribution it can make to the organisation.

Activities undertaken in public relations practice should follow from the organisation's objectives — supporting objectives should be set for these activities. Take as an example a major national airline like British Airways. Airlines have a number of important objectives relating to customers: potential customers have to be convinced that an airline like British Airways will provide safe, reliable, comfortable and enjoyable service. The airline's ultimate objectives are to serve more people, to retain and build its share of the market and to expand services. Public relations activities undertaken by the company are aimed at — internally — improving staff attitudes towards, and standards of service to, the customer; externally, activities are intended to develop relationships with potential customers so that they will wish to make use of the airline's services. Public relations activities are directed towards the achievement of specific objectives in these relationships and these are in turn derived from the organisation's overall objectives.

Public relations activities can also have a part to play in shaping organisational objectives, in several ways. First, information from the organisation's publics, fed back to the organisation in the course of public relations activities, may indicate that overall objectives are ill-founded. Second, in the course of trying to develop objectives for public relations activities, it may be found that organisational objectives are unclear, inconsistent with the organisation's actual behaviour — or non-existent. In each case, public relations has a part to play in helping to develop, re-shape or refine organisational objectives.

An example of how public relations may make this contribution to setting or changing an organisation's objectives is found in the experience of an electronics company involved in manufacturing systems for defence purposes (radar or weapons guidance systems, for example). Public relations activities which involve monitoring public and media opinion regarding company expansion plans might provide information which would influence the company's choice of a new location for a manufacturing plant. Modern public relations practice monitors public attitudes and opinions and summarises this information as 'intelligence', which is used to aid management decision making. Public relations practice, in its most developed form in commercial settings, is a process closely linked to senior management decision making, planning and objective setting. It is research based, drawing on surveys of opinions and attitudes and an analysis of trends in key relationships.

It also involves the anticipation of issues which may develop to disrupt important relationships. Anticipation leads companies to take what is sometimes described as a 'proactive' approach to public relations. In this approach, attempts are made to manage responses to issues before their impact is felt most strongly. This approach may also lead to attempts to influence legislation and setting of public policy, again before these have a harmful or undesired effect on the organisation's interests.

As a process, public relations involves research, planning, action and evaluation phases. The action phase involves communication, and is often mistaken for the whole of public relations practice. Communication is *the* major tool of public relations practice, but it must fit into a developed plan, aimed at specific publics and at the achievement of identified objectives. It must also be properly evaluated, through the use of formal or informal research techniques. These may include attitude and opinion research, media content analysis and work with focus groups.

As a task of management, public relations is necessary in large and small commercial organisations. The small, entrepreneurial business organisation must identify and manage key relationships in the same way as does the large multi-national company. Both depend on these key relationships for their viability. The small organisation depends on relations with financial institutions, customers, suppliers and local and trade publications; the larger organisation is also required to develop its relationships with comparable publics.

For the public sector, governmental or charitable organisation looking to the practice of public relations by commercial organisations for guidance, certain features stand out:

1. Commercial organisations must be competitive and sensitive to their customers' requirements. Public relations activities help to establish reputation and credibility, for organisations and for products. If properly managed and integrated with management planning and decision making, they do have the effect of making organisations more sensitive to the needs, expectations, opinions and attitudes of important publics.
2. Commercial pressures to minimise costs and maximise profits force business organisations to examine the costs of staffing and managing functions such as public relations. Major companies are often found to have small public relations staffs and, again, where the function is properly managed public relations activities will be evaluated in terms of the contribution they make to the achievement of organisational objectives.
3. The commercial practice of public relations leads to steady innovation in methods and techniques. Recent additions to practice — in issues management, in crisis communication and in the use of developments in evaluation techniques and communications technology — have had their origins in commercial experience.

Some of the lessons from commercial practice have been or are being adapted for use in public sector organisations. In the case of libraries, the commercial lesson of sensitivity to customer requirements and to public expectations is especially valuable. Libraries have relationships with a number of publics, including potential and actual users of library services (children and adult readers, for example), local government and its departments of social services, education and recreation, local interest groups, local and national associations. Libraries' broad objectives for their relationships with users seek to develop within them an understanding of library services and an enthusiasm for the use of those services.

Sensitivity to the customer requires library staff to put themselves in the place of the user. What are the users like? Old, young, well-educated, motivated — or unaware of library services? Answers to these questions can be derived from studies of actual users or from questioning new subscribers: how did they find out about library services? What newspapers or notices about library services do they see? Research can be formal, through questionnaires, or involve systematic questioning of users. Thinking about the important relationship with users can be informed by research, and realistic objectives can be set: for example, are too few young people using the library services, given the age profile of the population? If so, what objectives can be set to encourage more young people to join the library?

Another way of considering the user's point of view is to consider such basic questions as: is the library a welcoming place — colourful, warm and, to use a piece of computer jargon, 'user friendly'? Is it well signposted, so that the user can find parts of the library of interest? Are staff friendly and helpful — are the tasks of coming into the library, finding, choosing and taking out a book made easier by the service provided by staff? Are staff helpful when other library services are used?

Other relationships are of importance to libraries, of course. Local government provides funding: do local politicians and government officials understand the value of the services provided by the library? Will they be sufficiently informed to appreciate the need to maintain adequate funding for libraries? The media provide outlets for information about library services and events, through advertising and publicity. These relationships with government and the media must be managed so that funding remains at a realistic level for service to the public to be maintained and improved and so that the public is provided with adequate information about available services.

Increasingly, public sector organisations, health service organisations, or educational institutions are now expected to operate along more commercial lines. As they do so, the value of managed public relations activities will become more apparent. In future, public sector, governmental and charitable organisations will have to be more responsive to public expectations. They will have to devote more management time and effort to building important relationships with internal and external groups and will have to pay more attention to managed public relations activities.

REFERENCES
1. The corporate image: PR to the rescue. *Business Week*, 2569, January 22, 1979, 46-61.
2. Face the facts: freeze the tax. *Public Relations* (the Journal of the Institute of Public Relations), 6 (1), Autumn 1987, 17-19.

CHAPTER TWO
USER NEEDS

Colin Harris

It should go without saying that in both the ongoing promotion of a service and less regular campaigning an awareness is necessary of the needs of users and, in particular, how the needs of different types or groups of users differ from each other.

Library and information services are complex entities, as are the human users and potential users of those services. Nevertheless, when the erstwhile Centre for Research on User Studies (CRUS) was preparing a manual to assist public librarians in the analysis and profiling of their communities, a chief public librarian of a major English city is reported to have claimed not to need any such assistance. 'I know my users', he said, 'and I know their needs'.

This eminent librarian was talking nonsense. Of course, every librarian knows his or her users, to some extent. But two things limit the extent to which we can know our users through normal contact. One is that users are spread out; they may use different branches or departments or services. While librarians 'at the sharp end' may have substantial familiarity with their users, especially the very regular users, that does not produce the overview of users and their needs that is necessary for broader planning, promotion or campaigning. Secondly, it is in the nature of things that those whose needs we understand best are the very regular users, while those we wish to influence in promotion and campaigning are those who rarely or never use our services, and about whose needs we know very little.

Promotion and campaigning are but two activities in the broader exercise of marketing. Marketing, we have come to accept, means more than simply promotion and selling (metaphorically speaking, since what librarians in the public sector are selling is largely a 'free' service). Marketing is more broadly concerned with meeting users' needs. This may involve promoting existing products or services to markets with needs for those products or services but which are not currently using them; or it may involve identifying needs for new products, which may or may not exist among the users of existing products.

In marketing, the process of discovering untapped markets for existing products or services and of identifying needs for new products and services is called market research. Market research is simply the application of a range of social research techniques to the analysis of the needs and behaviours of users and potential users of products and services; in the library and information profession we have for years referred to these exercises as user studies.

A public library service, for example, is not really a single service at all, but a collection of a wide range of services, at the extremes quite different. There is also a wide variety of users, or of user groups. The fact that different user groups use different parts of the service has long been recognised by public librarians. There are children's libraries, for example, for use by children and an acknowledgement that adolescents have special needs and interests too, with specific provision for them. On the whole, however, the library is there to be used by anyone with a need and a wish to do so (subject, of course, to residence or membership).

In fact, of course, different parts of the service are designed for different parts of the community, and different parts of the community are likely to use different parts of the service. Anyone may borrow light fiction; anyone may make use of the technical reference library; anyone may make use of community information services. In practice, however, the three parts of the service are likely to be used, *on the whole*, by three different parts of the community. In promoting the library service, it is important to recognise this fact. Needs differ widely, and each service must be targeted at those with a need for it.

The difficulty lies in persuading those whom we believe have a need for a service that they actually do have a need for that service, and ought to use it (and, perhaps increasingly in the future, pay for it). Part of this difficulty in turn lies in the philosophical disagreement about whether or not one person (even a professional) can determine another person's needs (and tell them what they ought to do to resolve those needs). This problem is easily overcome. We simply have to persuade our users and potential users of the benefits of using our services to resolve their problems. But, to do that, we must know what those problems are.

STUDYING USERS' NEEDS

Studying users' needs is a complex task, partly because the needs themselves are complex. When we talk about 'information needs', for example, one of the difficulties is that, on the whole, users are not very good at articulating their needs for information, partly because needs are often characterised in terms of the solution to the need, and most users do not have a sophisticated appreciation of the range of solutions (e.g. different kinds of bibliographic tools, technology, the library and information network, etc.). On the other hand, some needs are quite easily expressed (e.g. longer opening hours, a wider range of new literature, less queuing at the reference desk, lower charges for inter-library loans).

Then there are some areas in which needs may be determined by the use of evaluative questions or expressions of opinion. It might be said here that, on the whole, it is better not to speak in terms of 'attitudes' to the library or information or whatever. Studying attitudes is a very complex task and, in any case, there is evidence that the link between people's expressed attitudes and their actual behaviour may be not very close.

To study users' needs, then, it may be necessary to use all three types of information — determinants of needs; expressed needs; and expressed opinions. Later in this chapter, we shall look at ways of eliciting this information. First, there are two general points to make about user studies.

The first is that there are various levels of contact with users that may be necessary. At one extreme, it is possible to study users' behaviour — not individually, but on aggregate — without reference to users at all. The use of a bookstock is best studied, not by studying users themselves but by studying the bookstock. The need for multiple copies of a book may be determined by the pattern of use of the stock, taking users' behaviour for granted. At a higher level, certain questions may be answered by the use of information about users that gets into the system without specifically asking them. For example, the residential location of users and the distances they travel to use a library may be taken into account in making decisions about opening new branch libraries. There are many other examples.[1] If, however, you wish to know what actually determines an individual's needs or behaviour, what they believe their needs to be, or what their evaluations or opinions are, then you must contact them directly.

Studying users' behaviour and gathering their opinions involves the use of the methods of social research. Here the librarian — or indeed anyone else without training or experience in social research but who needs to use its methods — faces a dilemma. On the one hand there are those who advise that some areas of social research amount to little more than common sense, while on the other there is a vast range of literature that implies that social research is an extremely technical activity not to be entered into by the uninitiated. This view appears to be reinforced by a belief that the more quantitative a study is, the more 'scientific' it is. This is not necessarily the case.

There is a limited number of ways in which information can be obtained from users. Basically, you can talk with them, directly or indirectly, or you can observe them. In social research terms, talking directly with users is done through interviews. This would normally be done face to face, although it is possible to do it remotely (by telephone, for example). Talking indirectly with users is done by questionnaire. You write down the questions; users write down the answers. Observation is observation.

Any of these methods can be used with varying degrees of structure. 'Structure' refers to three aspects of research:

— to the way in which questions are phrased,
— to the way in which answers may be expressed,
— to the sequence in which questions are asked.

Many people will have experience of highly structured interviews, in which the questions are always asked in a standard fashion (as it is written on the interview schedule), answers are allowed only in terms set by the interviewer (often in the form of supposedly mutually exclusive categories), and a standard sequence is used in asking the questions. An unstructured interview is much more like that which would be carried out by a television journalist. He will have a rough agenda of items about which he wishes to extract facts, explanations or opinions from the interviewee in the course of the interview. The questions will not be formulated in advance (he will have thought about them, but they do not have to be asked in any particular way); the interviewee is free, indeed must, answer in his own words; there is no pre-determined order of questions. The interview evolves as the interviewer and interviewee react in an unanticipatable way.

It is possible to use a 'semi-structured' approach, which may mean two things:
— the questioning itself may be semi-structured; for example the questions might be asked in a standard form, but the respondent allowed to answer in his own words.
— there may be a mixture of very structured and loosely structured questions.

The degree of structure that is used will depend very much on the purpose for which the research is being used. Sometimes you will have a very clear idea of what you want to know from a respondent, and also how you want the response expressed. For example, in a study of the use of the public library for technical information by local industry, you may wish to develop a basic profile of patterns of use. You may ask: "As far as you can recall, when was the last time you used the public library for technical information?" And the possible responses might be:
— Within the last 3 months
— Between 3 and 12 months ago
— More than 12 months ago
— or have you never used the public library for technical information?

The responses would aggregate in quite a straightforward way, and you would know exactly what they meant. (Unless, of course, the respondent had said something like "Well, it depends on what you mean by technical information".)

It may be the case that you are uncertain about precisely what questions you wish to ask, and do not want to constrain a respondent by using standard responses. If the area of study is new, or if you particularly wish to get the user's perspective (rather than simply the user's response to the librarian's perspective), then standardised questions and response categories will be inappropriate. Both the questioner and the respondent will need freedom to express themselves, to explore issues in ways that cannot be anticipated, etc. Again, your needs may be mixed.

On the actual techniques of data collection — interview, questionnaire, observation — there is a vast literature, including Maurice Line's excellent *Library surveys*[2] and the *CRUS Guides*,[3] both of which provide references to further sources. There are, however, one or two additional points to be made on methodology.

First to return to the dilemma faced by untrained or inexperienced researchers. Social research, including user studies, is a complex, technical activity. Textbooks written for students of social research are likely to include aspects that are not familiar to librarians contemplating research; the derivation of hypotheses from theory, the formulation of hypotheses and null hypotheses, ways of accepting or rejecting hypotheses, sampling, statistics, attitudes and their measurement, etc. Much of what is offered is often not relevant to librarians (nor, indeed to many other practising professionals, whose task is to improve their service, not to add to the development of social theory). On the other hand, some commentators like to treat social research methods as, for all practical purposes, more or less a matter of common sense. This is unhelpful and dangerous. While it may be the case that librarians can compromise their standards in some aspects of social research, they still have to be vigilant in others. The slightest carelessness in phrasing a question can produce a result from which it is impossible to make sense, so caution and thought are essential.

Second, in giving librarians advice on the technical aspects of user study design, it becomes clear that most librarians have given little thought to the objectives of their proposed project — what they want to find out, what they will do as a result of a particular finding, etc. It is common to start with questions like 'What questions should we include in the questionnaire?', 'How big a sample do we need?' etc. And questionnaires tend to grow and grow because there is no limit to the number of 'interesting' questions that users can be asked. If the objectives of a study are clear, much of the methodology follows logically.

Third, despite librarians' common recognition of their limited competence in statistics, there is an alarming tendency to regard *some* information as better than *none*. Those who favour 'quick and dirty' projects often seek to gather 'some' information — 'something to go on' — rather than be bothered with the technicalities and implications of such things as sample size and structure, response rate, etc. Sampling is an area that needs to be studied carefully if one is anxious to be able to treat results with statistical confidence. Suffice it to say here, that the larger the sample, the more confidently you can generalise from the sample to the population from which the sample is drawn (although huge samples are often a waste of resource). But a moment's thought will show that response rate is equally important. A large sample with a low response rate produces not only effectively a small sample, but also a biased sample. This is simply because those who respond may very well be, or are likely to be, different on the whole from those who do not. You would expect, for example, that those who are most appreciative or most critical of a service being studied, or most articulate or 'responsible', to respond. Those with less to say, for various reasons, will be less likely to respond. Not only will the responses give an unbalanced picture of the population as a whole, but it may even be the non-respondents that it is most important to know about.

THE USE OF USER STUDIES AND THEIR RESULTS

As was suggested earlier, user studies have a very wide range of uses in relation to the promotion and marketing of a service:

(i) they may be used for purely descriptive purposes, to answer questions about the characteristics of people using or not using various parts of a service.

(ii) they may be used to evaluate new services or innovations. 'Did a user education programme result in greater or different use of the service?', 'Is the Small Business Information Service a more effective way of meeting the needs of small business?', etc. Such studies may require 'before and after' studies, or at least the availability of some data on the 'before' position. For example, if you wanted an objective measure of the level of use by a particular group before a user education programme, you would have to satisfy yourself that such data could be produced. Such an approach might not be necessary. In the other example, the evaluation of a business information service, comparison with the 'before' position would be provided by respondents as part of the study.

(iii) they may be used to identify needs for existing services. Perhaps the most common outcome of studies of users' needs and behaviour is the identification of needs that can be met by currently available services or products. It is common in small businesses, for example, for people to flounder around for a long time, after making extensive enquiries among friends and colleagues, looking for basic information that is available from a directory or handbook on the public library shelves. In marketing existing products and services, the public library has many obstacles to overcome:

— the library's image may make it hard for many in business and industry to grasp that the public library can make a contribution to innovation, productivity or problem solving. The public library may be seen as a leisure service or as support for formal study, local history, etc.

— equally, the library's image may make it hard for educationally or otherwise disadvantaged groups to grasp that the public library can do something for them.

- the public library will increasingly have to persuade its users and potential users not only that use of library services may be beneficial but also that it is worth paying for.
- the public library is not the only source of information in people's lives. There are many other sources of information, formal and informal, free and priced, good quality and bad quality. It is particularly significant that people use information sources that are easy to use rather than those that will deliver the best information. The public library has to decide with which other information sources or agencies it wishes to compete. This is a crucial question, both in promotion and campaigning.

(iv) finally, user studies may be used to identify needs for new products or services. This is an area fraught with difficulty. Some needs ought to be easily identifiable. For example, it is easy for users to express a need for longer opening hours, more branches, lower prices for charged services, etc., but that is not the same as *using* those services. Trial services and/or choices have to be made. The task of identifying genuinely new products or services is harder still; since needs are so often expressed in terms of solutions, it is that much harder to express a need in the absence of a solution to that need. The hardest task in the development of new products and services, however, lies in the tension between what users *like* to do and what librarians think users *ought* to do. The choice is between developing products, services and systems that neglect how users actually behave and developing systems that librarians think are proper and then trying to persuade users to adapt to them.

This is not the place to review the results of the large number of public library user studies that have been conducted over the years. Many factors, such as changing demographic patterns, changing patterns of employment and education, changing socio-economic behaviour from car and telephone ownership to book-buying habits, changes in technology, etc., will have rendered many past findings no longer relevant. On the other hand, some of the generalisations mentioned earlier probably still stand: people prefer to use information that is easily obtained (local, informal, verbal); they are, on the whole, ignorant of the formal information system and what it can deliver; there are many barriers to the effective use of public libraries; a substantial proportion of the population will never perceive the public library as relevant to their needs; etc.

User studies have a proper place in the development of library services and in their promotion and the contribution that they make to the understanding of different users groups' behaviour and needs can assist effective campaigning. It is clear, however, that interpreting the results of user studies and acting upon them are problematic. The problems can be partly resolved by developing user studies from clear objectives for the exercise and a consideration before the study takes place of how the results might be acted upon, rather than starting with a long list of 'interesting questions'.

It has to be remembered, however, that if a campaign wants to be able to claim or demonstrate that, for example, x% or most of the population are delighted with their library service, a user study specifically designed to produce such evidence may be treated with suspicion. The campaigning use of user studies may be much more opportunistic and, as well as using user studies produced within the library, it may be helpful to compare the local situation with that evidenced by user studies in other authorities.

REFERENCES
1. See for example: CHESHIRE COUNTY COUNCIL RESEARCH AND INTELLIGENCE SECTION. *Methods of study: methods of studying library use and attitudes.* Chester: Cheshire County Council, 1985.
2. LINE, M.B. *Library surveys: an introduction to the use, planning procedure and presentation of surveys.* 2nd ed. London: Bingley, 1982.
3. STONE, S. and HARRIS, C. *CRUS Guide 1: designing a user study, general research design.* Sheffield: University of Sheffield Centre for Research on User Studies, 1984.

    STONE, S. and HARRIS, C. *CRUS Guide 2: basic social research techniques.* Sheffield: University of Sheffield Centre for Research on User Studies, 1984.

    STONE, S. and HARRIS, C. *CRUS Guide 3: analysing data.* Sheffield: University of Sheffield Centre for Research on User Studies, 1984.

    STONE, S. and HARRIS, C. *CRUS Guide 4: writing research reports.* Sheffield: University of Sheffield Centre for Research on User Studies, 1984.

    HEATHER, P. and STONES, S. *CRUS Guide 5: questionnaires.* Sheffield: University of Sheffield Centre for Research on User Studies, 1984.

    STONE, S. *CRUS Guide 6: interviews.* Sheffield: University of Sheffield Centre for Research on User Studies, 1984.

    MULLINGS, C. *CRUS Guide 7: observation.* Sheffield: University of Sheffield Centre for Research on User Studies, 1984.

CHAPTER THREE
PLANNING A CAMPAIGN: PUBLIC LIBRARIES
Joe Hendry

When I was first appointed Chief Librarian at Renfrew, in November 1974, it was not my intention merely to pick up the reins, so to speak, of the merging library authorities, bring these together, and allow these library services to carry on as they had prior to the re-organisation of local government in Scotland. I considered that I wanted to see the new public library service at Renfrew to be at the centre of local government and not, as so often seemed the case, on the periphery. I also wanted to see the vast majority of the local populace using the libraries on a regular basis. I therefore formulated a planned strategy to achieve this.

It is my firm belief that in planning a campaign there must be an underlying sense of purpose, of belief not only in what you want to achieve, but why you want to achieve it in the first place. If there is no underlying sense of philosophy and of belief, I consider it would be impossible to develop positive public services, in particular though not only, in local government. Therefore a sense of belief is the bedrock which such a campaign requires. If staff are convinced that this Belief is *their* belief, then you have the opportunity to motivate, to create common attitudes, and the beginnings of a common culture. In this case I believed very firmly that public libraries were, potentially, very relevant and very important to the everyday lives of ordinary people. Yet at that time less than 25% of Renfrew's population of 210,000 were regular library users. So the first step in my strategy was to think through, carefully and coherently, and to commit to paper, what I believed public libraries were for — their purpose. It seems to me that in planning any campaign it is necessary to communicate at an early stage with those with whom you would work, and to convince them that, collectively, something important and significant is developing, and that it is made quite clear to them what is expected of them, and the contribution they would make. I therefore stated what I saw as the basic principles of a public library service. These were as follows:

Aims and Objectives: To promote the spread of knowledge, information, education and culture by:
(i) stimulating intellectual, artistic and imaginative activity, and encouraging and fostering leisure interests.

(ii) acting as a counter-balance to the excesses of other forms of mass media, by representing in library book stocks all shades of moral, religious and political opinion; by making the resources of the library free to all sections of the community; and by ensuring maximum individual choice for all members of the community.
(iii) acting as the collective memory of the community by storing ideas, information and the imaginative creations of mankind.
(iv) acting as the custodian of all materials such as books, pamphlets, newspapers, archives, photographs, relating to the history and contemporary life of the community which the libraries serve.

These were sent with a covering letter to every member of staff. There were no instructions in the letter. Its theme was to tell our staff what I believed in, what I wanted them to share with me, and how I believed we could work towards a positive and special end. At the same time I placed these objectives before the District Council for approval. I thus had a beginning, namely a common *credo,* translated into clear aims and objectives.

Public library services are, by their very nature, scattered and sometimes isolated not only from each other, but from much of the rest of local government. There will always be particular problems of communication, because of the very nature of the services we provide. To harness the particular attributes and characteristics of each service point (I do not care for the term *branch* library) it is necessary not only to have this common set of beliefs; it also requires a formalised and planned structure which allows a physically scattered service to work as an integrated one.

I consider that the three basic components in a public library service are books, public and staff, and that the catalyst which brings the public and the books together is the staff. My thoughts in this respect have always been close to those of the library philosophy of S.R. Ranganathan. Again, he continually argued for a library philosophy. As these were the three components, I proposed a staff structure based on this perceived situation. This is a crucial part in the basic planning of a campaign. We require a coherent structure within which people involved in a campaign can work together in a way that allows them to relate to each other, and to other aspects and areas of the service, beyond that in which they themselves are involved. Such a structure must be flexible and allow integration, rather than the hierarchical bureaucracies which plague and debilitate many organisations, especially it seems, public services.

For example I have seen many public library systems where lending services, reference services, and centralised support and administrative services find it very difficult to communicate across the barriers created by a hierarchical staff structure. Only on a personal basis do individuals communicate across such obstacles. I have been told that it is in the inherent nature of such services that one component, such as lending services, is often not aware of what is happening in another, such as reference services. In my view the reason for this is a bad management structure. An integrated matrix structure, based on an accurate assessment of the underlying key components in any organisation, allows a much more flexible, planned approach to launching a planned campaign.

The first three steps in planning a campaign in a public library context are, therefore:
(i) knowing what your beliefs are, and therefore what you want to achieve;
(ii) communicating these beliefs as practical objectives, to the people with whom you must work, in order that these objectives can be fulfilled;
(iii) creating a vehicle which allows this to happen, and this can only be achieved by defining the basic components and organising them in such a way that the whole is greater than the sum of the parts.

I am aware that such a progression might seem a rather simplistic one. It is intended to be so. Any organisation, any campaign, requires that lines of work, of communication, are kept 'clean', i.e. clear and well-defined.

The next step is to ensure that the inevitable bureaucracy will run as smoothly as possible. Again this comes back to 'clean' lines. In this case, that the rules and regulations in existence are meant to encourage the use of the public library service rather than hinder the development of a much broader level of public use. Any library campaign, be it a major, ambitious and long-term one such as Renfrew embarked on in 1974, or a more modest one in a specific locality, aimed at a specific clientele, such as children, will not succeed if the rules and regulations in the libraries service, and the manner of implementation by staff, are counter-productive to and militate against the agreed objectives of the campaign.

In Renfrew there are no fines or request charges. We considered that there were more negative public relations situations generated in libraries by arguments and resentments relating to fines than to any other regulations. We also thought that fines and request charges discouraged precisely those whom we had already defined in our aims and objectives as those whom we most wanted to encourage to use our libraries, i.e. the poor, the unemployed, the lower income groups who traditionally do not use our services on a consistent basis. Part of our planning process therefore, was to reduce these rules and regulations to a minimum, and make it quite clear to the librarians in the community that they, as the people on the spot, had the responsibility to take decisions; ultimately, to use *their* discretion.. To give people at the local level a broad range and depth of responsibilities, within a clearly defined structure, but especially, within the context of a common culture, a common set of values and beliefs, is the vehicle by which the implementation of such a campaign can be established.

The next step is to gather the necessary and accurate management information required if we are to respond to the public's needs. Issue statistics are useful as an indicator, but only that, and if they are not accurate they can be downright dangerous. I remember computerising libraries in Renfrew at re-organisation, only to discover to my horror that the real issue levels were 10% lower than the manual records of issues had previously shown. Input and output measurements are a topic for a separate essay, but we must be clear that we are obtaining the accurate information we need. For example, do we know, in any given, defined community, the demographic make-up of that community and how that relates to the use of the local library; equally do we know the socio-economic groupings in that community?

In relation to stock, are we aware what parts of this stock are most popular, and what proportion is not used by the public? If it's not what the public want and need, then you will never increase the number of people using the service. In order to provide materials which people will read, and want to read, on a consistent basis, it is an axiom that the staff must know both their stock and their public, at a local level. That is the reason why it is so important to make it quite clear that it is the local community librarian who has the responsibility for the running of the library in that community, the selection (and rejection) of stock, and the authority to take decisions and to implement policies, without a continual need to seek higher authority, or to be stultified and frustrated by a central bureaucracy which may consider itself, and the individuals in it, as more expert and more significant than those library workers operating at local community level.

If the logic of a policy aimed to increase the number of people using library services is to provide what people want and need, then libraries can clearly provide a whole range of information and activities. Perhaps a useful 'rule of thumb' assessment of relevant management information is to assess the various reasons why people have come into libraries. A campaign such as Renfrew's, therefore, had to (a) define geographically and managerially how policies were to be effected and by whom; in essence by decentralisation to community level of as much professional decision-making as possible, while (b) ensuring that as many administrative details were removed from the local librarian's back, both in terms of simplifying the regulations and centralising the ordering and distribution (but *not* the selection) of materials.

Renfrew's campaign had, therefore, in a planned twelve-month period developed a culture (in a management sense) amongst its staff, by providing the belief, the practical objectives; staff structure; and the subsequent decentralisation of decision-making and responsibilities. In any campaign, of any length, there comes a time to take stock, to review the situation. You have to examine the direction in which you chose to steer this campaign, and to what extent, at various levels, it has been successful, *up to that point in the campaign.* You must then decide whether the direction remains correct in the light of experience, and then whether a fundamental review of this strategy is required or only minor improvements and adjustments.

In Renfrew by that time our registered readers had increased from 25% of the population to 48%; in parallel our issues had increased from 1.4 million books per year, to 3.2 millions. In making this assessment after this first twelve months, we concluded that our initial strategy had been correct, but recognised that we had adopted policies which were being implemented with a fairly broad brush. Our assessment for the next twelve to thirty-six months was that although the agreed direction should still be adhered to, that much more than minor adjustments were required. Rather, that selected targeting of particular groups and in particular geographical areas, was now needed.

It had become quite clear that the substantial increase in levels of use was not a uniform one. The largest rises in numbers of registered readers, in books issued, in requests and reservations, and in the sheer volume of people coming into libraries for a wide variety of reasons, was most marked in those libraries which might be termed town centre libraries, *viz.* Paisley Central Library, and those in the town centres of Johnstone, Barrhead and Renfrew. The increased levels of use in the housing schemes were less than in this first category. Equally, we identified a number of communities in the District (Renfrew District covers 150 square miles and has a wide range of urban and rural communities) which had no reasonable library service within walking distance, and in some cases, no library service at all.

We therefore produced a series of reports and assessments of needs in these areas, for consideration by the District Council, for insertion in their Five Year Capital Building Programme. In any organisation there are, inevitably, competing interests for limited resources. We therefore had to maximise our case to the public, but especially to the District Council. In order to do so, we had to convince those who took decisions about resources, especially financial allocations, that our Libraries Service was a positive one, and was politically relevant and important to the people whom councillors represented. We therefore tried to gauge what was of most concern to councillors, and to much of the general public.

It took no great imagination to see that the spectre of growing unemployment was causing increasing worry and concern throughout many parts of West Central Scotland, including Renfrew. We believed that libraries had a positive contribution to make in this circumstance and we therefore came to an agreement with the local job centres to display job cards in our local libraries; to offer help and advice to those seeking employment or re-training; to allow free use of telephones, typewriters, advice on framing applications and filling in forms; and in providing a wide-ranging and up-to-date collection of information relating to jobs and careers, at every library service point. We recognised that if this stimulated the demand which we hoped, that we had to be prepared for our new users. We therefore increased our seating accommodation, provided a wider range of newspapers and periodicals, substantially increased our paperback collections, and took steps to ensure that local libraries and job centres were capable of providing this job information by means of daily updated job cards. Basically, we had come to the point in our long term strategy where we were stimulating substantial demands and expectations. We now had to ensure that we could not only meet these demands, but continue to deliver a high level of service on a regular basis. In one Paisley community library, in the isolated Foxbar Housing Scheme, the number of adult registered readers increased by 14% in the first three-month period after job cards and related information were introduced there.

In parallel with this, there were three other aspects to this strategy:
(i) to be seen to be positive and successful in the eyes of decision makers;
(ii) and by those who influenced these decision makers;
(iii) to provide a tangible and highly relevant service to those in the decision-making process.

Senior officers and elected members in local government are extremely busy people, and have little time for study, quiet reflection or recreational reading. In short, they would not have time to use local libraries on a regular and conventional basis and thus appreciate the improved quality of this service, or its increasing levels of use by the general public. However they did, and do, have a great need for up-to-date, relevant information in the fields where they have responsibilities, and equally, they examine the local press in great detail as they consider that local newspapers carry significant influence in their town, burgh or ward. We therefore needed to develop our information services to local government; and in parallel, we needed a clearly-defined policy for the Libraries Service, in relation to the local press and the regional and national media.

First, therefore, we proposed to the District Council that we establish a Local Government Library and Information Unit based in the municipal buildings and located immediately adjacent to the Council committee rooms and debating chamber. This would provide a wide range of political, financial and current affairs material in book and periodical form, together with a wide range of textbooks and other background material for the various professional disciplines in local government. Most importantly, we produced a fortnightly list of current items with brief abstracts. This *Bulletin* was circulated to all elected members, senior officers, and all departments. The new service was heavily used from the outset, and it soon became apparent that a number of key decision-makers had altered their perceptions of the range of the Library Service's work and influence.

Secondly, we had taken great care to get to know the local newspaper personnel, the personalities, interests and styles; the level at which these newspapers were written, circulation, deadlines, policies on photographs, and in general how the editors and journalists saw their target audience. Local newspapers have one very obvious strength, if handled properly: quite simply, they are *local* and cultivate a local sense of identity between the newspaper and the readers in the local community.

The senior management in the Libraries Service decided therefore, that our strategy would be to attempt to have fairly small, positive 'pieces' appear on a regular basis, on the inside pages of the local press; that we would produce short informative press releases, no more than three paragraphs, only on one page, and carrying a short one-line caption, and a name, address and 'phone number as a contact for further information. We therefore organised a series of briefing sessions for our local community librarians so they were quite clear what was expected of them, namely, if it was a local event or competition they drafted their press release early, knew when it had to arrive in the local newspaper offices so it was in time to catch the appropriate deadline, without either arriving far too early and therefore being lost, or arriving too late to be included. A copy had also to reach senior management at the same time. It is vital in this situation that 'one hand knows what the other is doing'. Local papers use a lot of photographs, especially group photographs. If the local press wouldn't send a photographer to cover an event, we told our staff to take their own photographs in black and white, get them developed in twenty-four hours, and deliver photographs and copy to the local press by hand, immediately thereafter. And not just to the person at reception, but have a named journalist in mind.

The result of this policy was, and has been consistently since, that the library service and its activities receive a consistently middle-key, positive image, which builds up a long term impression both amongst the general public and decision-makers of a positive and locally relevant service. A group photograph of fifty young children, all with teddy bears, surrounding the local councillor (who is of course judging the local library's Teddy Bear Competition) and which is featured in the centre pages of the local paper, is — wonderful. And no child goes home without some small prize or gift. We believed that the attention to that type of detail was crucial to the success of a positive public relations policy.

Thirdly, we recognised that local authorities and local people feel that their community is something rather special, and that they feel a great sense of satisfaction in having this recognised beyond the local community. Therefore in any planned campaign, a policy and a strategy for relating to the regional media has an important complementary role to the local strategy which I have outlined above in my first and second points. Many areas outwith the large cities can even feel aggrieved at being consistently ignored by the regional media such as local radio, the regional press, and television. Therefore if a service such as Libraries has something positive to publicise, in highlighting its local community activities to a wider audience, perhaps several times a year, this will likely have an important impact on the local community and its decision makers.

Once again, you require to consider this from a journalist's standpoint: twists, angles, type of copy, deadlines, who the paper is aimed at (very often the regional newspapers tend to be aimed at a middle-class readership, and such newspapers are more in touch, so we are told, with what middle-class, decision-makers want). If that is the case, and I believe that substantially it is, then it is particularly important to propagate a positive image, publicised in such a way that it will be of wider, regional interest.

Equally, interviews on radio have the same effect. The situation however in television is something rather different. It is normally extremely difficult to obtain coverage on television, even in regional, minority programmes such as 'The Arts', 'Books', and so on. What a library publicist has to remember, however, is never to forget or lose touch with any contacts you have made in the past, in any of these fields, but especially television. If you have the name of a researcher, producer or editor, send your copy there, and if you are serious about coverage, be prepared to drop everything for the television cameras. Further, recognise you will only be on for a few minutes, so when you are briefed by an interviewer, know the areas of questioning which you want to have asked of you; suggest these as perhaps being of some help to the interviewer, and make sure your physical appearance is neat, tidy and business-like. If you send a press release to television, make sure that you have a reasonably smart suit, dress, or other appropriate outfit available, just in case you get the call. Those who turn up in horn-rimmed spectacles, hairy jackets and scuffed suede shoes should never ever again complain about the unfairness of the image projected by the media, of us as individual librarians, and of the library profession.

In situations where you have been interviewed on radio or television, try and have this interview taped or video recorded, then examine this recording for the positive and negative aspects of your interview; resolve never to make the mistakes again, and practise, practise and re-practise. It can be a chastening experience to watch or listen to your 'performance' on tape, but do not shirk it. You learn by studying your tapes, learning from your mistakes and remembering that if you are going to propagate your service, then you must recognise and learn from these experiences.

We believe in the intrinsic value of libraries in the pursuit of knowledge and the provision of information. We owe it to ourselves, our profession, but especially our library services, to be coherent and skilled in our capacity to project ourselves, and therefore our service, in a positive and skilled way.

PLANNING A CAMPAIGN

Last of all, especially in relation to television, pick your news release carefully, and only send the occasional one (perhaps four per year) that have the potential interest for television journalists. Nevertheless, in all aspects of radio, television and the press, the journalists and researchers whom you attempt to influence, will likely be middle-class and library users; certainly, readers who are often highly articulate and positive about books and libraries. As this sympathy tends to be there from the start, my advice to you is to use this.

In the thirty-six month period after our first year's operation, our Libraries Service was featured on television once each year, culminating in the award of 'Scottish Consumer Champion' in December 1979, this award being given by the Scottish Consumer Council and publicised through their own very professional press officer. In that period on radio we also featured 'Adult Literacy', 'Job Cards', 'Community Information', the 'Urgent Needs of the Unemployed', 'What People are Reading', the 'Advent of New Technology and Computers in Libraries', and a number of related topics. In all we were featured nineteen times on radio in the first four years of our operation. We also booked two advertisements in the local commercial radio station, Radio Clyde. We booked a series of ten spots highlighting our Easter Bunny children's competitions — held in every library in our system — as a focus on children's activities during Easter holiday week. We also booked a block of ten adverts for adult consumption, simply stressing that 'Your public library provides books, newspapers, periodicals, records and tapes'; that the library service is provided by the community for the individuals in it, to use for their benefit; that this service is available to everyone and that there are no registration fees or charges. It ended by stressing that 'Your library service belongs to you'. The reaction from our public at library service points was very positive, and as I had discovered that Radio Clyde was piped into the Linwood car factory during the night shift, we were putting our message over to a lot of people. As a result of this, our library at Linwood increased its number of registered readers and its issues substantially. This also had the further advantage that, having spent money at Radio Clyde, this radio station seemed thereafter to be particularly sympathetic to Renfrew District Libraries Service.

As a result of this campaign, and the forward planning which we had laid down to allow us to cope with and react positively to the demand we had stimulated, two other factors were necessary: first, that we could prove that we should have a Books and Related Materials Fund which would increase in *real* terms each year, in order to meet rising levels of use; and secondly, that a 'rolling programme' of new and converted libraries be included in the District Council's Capital Building Programme. Between 1975 and 1985 Renfrew Libraries opened ten new or converted service points, and introduced two mobile library services (there had been no previous history of mobiles in Renfrewshire).

By 1985 the level of registered readers in Renfrew was 67% of the population, on a computerised system whereby if an enrolled reader did not use the library service for one year, he or she automatically came off the register; the number of books issued had risen to 3.7 million per year, the number of volunteers coming forward to help with the Housebound Service had trebled in ten years; further, an atmosphere had been created where a series of innovative projects had been established such as the Linwood Information Project (LINFO), which is a one-door approach to local government services, giving advice and information on a wide range of matters, especially financial, to the people not only of Linwood, but to the District as a whole, and beyond; the Ferguslie Park Project, which introduced a completely new kind of public library service in one of the most deprived housing schemes in Western Europe, with an active Users' Group, Library Youth Workers, and an ambitious outreach programme, especially concerning money-related matters and benefits; Johnstone Information and Leisure Library (JILL), is one of Britain's first separate libraries planned for teenagers, especially unemployed young people (in a town where youth unemployment stands at over 90%).

These projects could not have been introduced without a consistently high standard of public library provision throughout the Library Service, combined with an equally high standard of planned public relations, consistently adhered to over a ten year campaign. Nor would they have been such an outstanding success in terms of service delivery to the public, without the hard work, attention to detail, but equally important, as a result of the confidence which was brought about by an underlying philosophy, a collective sense of staff 'culture' and commitment, and a confidence which comes from a recognition and a pride in one's contribution to a local community. Also, the confidence to exercise flair, vivacity and a little imagination.

In 1986 Renfrew's Libraries Service was awarded the Library Association's Robinson Gold Medal for Library Innovation for the work of the Teenage Library (JILL); in 1987 this Service was awarded the overall runners-up Public Relations Award in the Library Association T.C. Farries Public Relations Awards. The Service's Chief Librarian was awarded the personal Public Relations Award in the same year, for services to the library profession.

The present period has been one in which the Libraries Service has once again required to take stock of its effectiveness. There are several reasons for this: first it was time again to examine our circumstances and consider if our strategy required to change, and if so, to what degree; secondly, the financial constraints on local government make it almost impossible to continue to develop services, and this has in itself resulted, in its more positive aspects, in an attempt to consolidate, retrench and re-examine not only our service, but the changes in society, its standards, values and expectations, the continuing and insidious blight of unemployment, and the impact of new technology and increased leisure. The service is now at a new crossroads, in part because of these factors, but also because the Libraries Service is now to be the core and largest part of a new department, Arts and Cultural Services, within the District Council. This new service will also include museums, art galleries, community centres and halls, town halls, a new Paisley Arts Centre, and the development of a community arts policy.

It is time therefore, for a fundamental re-think of these new and existing relationships, for a re-assessment of priorities, service delivery, image and style. The beginnings of a new public relations campaign are beginning to emerge. First, I believe that many of us in Renfrew's Service have now become too entrenched and we perhaps need an external Public Relations Adviser to help us to think laterally and afresh; coupled with this we should be preparing to embark on a policy planning exercise to enable us to re-assess our priorities and effectiveness against our resources (people, materials, buildings, money and goodwill). Perhaps the ultimate lesson to be learned in planning a publicity campaign is that it never ends. And that is how it should be. There will, too, be many criticisms of those who seek to develop a positive public relations campaign. If you suffer much unfair criticism, remember that Cicero had the rights of it, when he wrote:

> Upon the very books in which philosophers bid us scorn ambition, they inscribe their names. They seek publicity for themselves on the very page where they pour contempt upon publicity.
>
> CICERO *Pro Archia Poeta*. Chapter 11, sect. 26

CHAPTER FOUR
PLANNING A CAMPAIGN: THE SPECIAL LIBRARY AND INFORMATION SERVICE
Sylvia P. Webb

Why do special libraries exist? There is certainly no legal requirement such as that by which public libraries must be provided, neither is such provision required by company law. But special libraries, information services, information units, do exist and continue to be set up. In certain fields, for example legal firms, they have come to be seen as an outstanding example of a growth area. However, like any other product or service their existence does not guarantee their continuance, or right to it. They must have a purpose which is clearly identifiable, not only to those specialists working within the department, but to the rest of the organisation.

The reason for the establishment of the initial service may well have been described originally in broad terms, for example 'to set up a central collection of information' or more specifically, 'to provide research facilities and services for managers'. These statements say nothing about the objectives of the service, nor the means by which they will be achieved, i.e. what the service does, and what it is capable of doing. It is this that everyone in the organisation needs to know if the full potential of the service is to be realised, and its continuance assured.

A special library should not be seen as a centre where information is merely held or accessed, but one from which active dissemination of information emanates. It is capable of making a considerable contribution to a whole range of its parent organisation's activities. If it does this effectively, it will be operating as a key function within the organisation. To achieve this, library and information staff need to maintain a constant awareness of the changing objectives of the organisation, so that they can make essential and timely contributions on an ongoing basis. They also need to ensure that they are seen in this broader role, so that they automatically receive all necessary internal information. To quote from a paper produced by the Special Libraries Section of the Library Association of Australia, South Australia Branch:

> Special libraries are not so-called simply because of the specialised nature of their collections. Such libraries also have a special relationship with their users. It is an axiom of special librarianship that the material should reach the client before it is asked for. This anticipatory role relies

upon the librarian's close and continuous contact with the library's clientele and their current interests.[1]

Already we have a number of concepts on the table for discussion — perception, expectation, communication. These are all influences which need to be considered before any promotion of the service can take place. Publicising the service is just one part of the marketing strategy, which must be well thought out before any promotion activities can take place. What is required to develop the marketing strategy? A realistic, well-structured plan with clearly stated objectives and, equally important, well-defined methods. If we look at the main activities involved in carrying out the marketing plan we will see where promotion sits, and the evaluation which is necessary to provide the basis on which promotional activities can be built and from which they can be implemented. Promotion, publicity and public relations involve much more than just slick presentation.

ORGANISATIONAL INFLUENCES

This leads back to the initial question:- Why does the special library (or more specifically, your particular library) exist? Until this question is answered, you will be unable to address the issue of promotion. So the first step is to establish the current purpose of the service as it is seen by the rest of the organisation. What is management's expectation of the library and information service? Has it been clearly stated and on what is it based?

If you are in the business of promoting a new service, one which you are in the process of setting up, you will have had to establish what the expectations of management are in order to commence the setting up process. This will have given you a useful picture of the organisation, its structure and hierarchy. It can then begin to be viewed as a target group or series of groups, and the style of the promotion campaign structured accordingly. It is essential that a full understanding of the organisation's internal politics is gained if successful promotion and an appropriate plan for the service's future development is to be achieved. It must also be remembered that promotion is not a one-off event but a continuous process. Not only is it essential to acquire an understanding of the internal politics, but in addition it is necessary to look at the organisation's place in the external environment. What are its relationships with other organisations? How do these influence its information needs?

The organisation as an entity dictates the direction of your service in a variety of ways. Apart from policy and procedural matters such as finance and staffing, which apply across the board, the physical setting in which you operate has a strong influence on the display and effective exploitation of your resources. The building in which you are located, its ease of access, its visibility, the equipment and furniture, the arrangement of stock, all have a dramatic effect on the way in which the overall service is perceived. Another equally important part of the visual presentation is of course the image projected by the staff.

STAFF ATTITUDES AND TRAINING

Staff attitudes and expectations are crucial; the objectives of the service and its role within the organisation need to be clearly defined and stated at an early stage of the individual's employment with the department. Induction training would be the obvious starting place for this, and it should be a regular discussion point in any subsequent training programme.

'How can we best handle this?' should be the question at the forefront of the staff approach. The emphasis here is on 'we' and 'best' — a co-ordinated team acting to agreed standards will provide a high quality of service. The word 'this' is also important as it suggests the need to consider each requirement individually and adapt accordingly, thus further suggesting flexibility of approach. The staff represent the service. However comprehensive the sources of information may be, they are unlikely to be fully exploited, or the service seen as a key business function, without the positive contribution of the personalities and skills of the staff. It is these which most strongly project the image of the service. As Ray Prytherch says in his Introduction to *Staff training in libraries,* 'effective staff do not happen, they must be created through training'.[2]

In the training programme which I drew up for information staff at Stoy Hayward, there was as much emphasis on management and interpersonal skills, as on information skills. This balance is essential if an effective service is to be developed and offered on a continuing basis, particularly in the special library setting where constant change is part of daily life. The Stoy Hayward training programme, which is set out in *Personal development in information work,*[3] includes one-day courses on, for example, presentation skills, report writing and rapid reading, all of which provide an excellent training for such specific areas of library activity as user education; presentation of the findings of desk research; the preparation of budget and other management reports, and abstract-writing and scanning, as well as promotion activities.

At Stoy Hayward we were fortunate in having these particular courses available in-house, but similar courses are offered externally, by a number of training companies and consultants, such as those listed in the *Management training directory.*[4] The Library Association is currently expanding its range of continuing education courses in these sorts of areas. Task Force Pro Libra now backs up its recruitment activities with management courses designed specifically with the needs of the library and information professional in mind, as does Aslib.

PLANNING A CAMPAIGN

EFFECTIVE COMMUNICATION

Communication skills are central to all information work. The whole enquiry process is based on communication. Between the initial request for information, and the ultimate presentation of that information back to the enquirer, a whole series of different communication processes such as the following take place:
— eliciting the actual requirement from the client
— discussing the approach with colleagues
— seeking expert opinion from other departments in-house
— making contact with potential external sources of information, either by some form of telecommunication, or by personal visits
— analysing the results of the search
— presenting the final outcome to the enquirer.

That is a simple example and does not attempt to look into all the complex communication manoeuvres which take place during what might at first sight seem to be a straightforward routine part of daily information work. Yet, although overtly this is part of the information seeking and retrieving process, each step also forms part of the all-important second agenda aimed at promoting the service. Every piece of communication is a form of client contact and as such says something about the person transmitting the various messages and the department which he or she represents. To the outside world there is an additional responsibility as a representative of the overall organisation. The simple act of picking up the telephone requires considerable forethought and training if best use is to be made of it. A clear speaking voice is certainly essential, but so too is the ability to structure the message in concise, unambiguous terms, and to know when to terminate the conversation.

The telephone is a central feature of special library work, often being much more the usual method of contact by the enquirer than the personal visit, particularly where the client may be situated on a site other than that on which the library is located. The fee-based Biomedical Information Service of the University of Minnesota's Bio-Medical Library found this to be an important consideration when offering their services externally.[5] In industrial and commercial libraries you would rarely ask the client to stay on the line unless an immediate answer was possible. It is much more likely that you would note the details, preferably on a pre-printed form to save time, and return the enquirer's call as soon as the information became available. Such an approach saves the enquirer time and projects a business-like image of the information service and staff. Telephone training is an essential requirement for all staff if a consistently positive and efficient image is to be maintained. General practical advice on telephone technique is given in the Industrial Society's booklet *Guide to telephone techniques*.[6]

Telephone interaction is an example of verbal communication, one which is not just concerned with the enunciation of words. Rather, it should be seen as a tool, which requires careful thought before use, but which if used skilfully can produce very positive results. Verbal communication is that which involves the use of words. Apart from the spoken word, other examples of verbal communication would include written communications, such as reports, reviews, newsletters etc. Verbal communication can be divided under two broad headings, under which examples are given as follows:

oral/aural:
- meetings, talks, visits
- informal contact — telecommunications

written:
- progress reports/reviews
- annual reports
- budget and development proposals
- newsletters/bulletins
- minutes/agendas
- personnel documentation.

Non-verbal communication is concerned with the transmission of messages without using words. This can include the use of sounds which may be commonly accepted as word replacements e.g. 'm'mm' often replaces 'yes'. These can also stand on their own if uttered in a particular way, e.g. 'oohs' and 'aahs' can express surprise, pleasure or pain depending on the voice inflection. Non-verbal communication includes posture, appearance, eye-contact, gesture, facial expression, signals, rituals.

Signals such as pointing and rituals like the handshake, also act as verbal replacements, but all these depend on a knowledge and understanding of the accepted norms in the particular culture in which we find ourselves. It is therefore essential to know the rules which operate in each organisation. Facial expression and gestures add a lot to both the spoken word and to word replacements. To see just how much, why not study the non-verbal aspects of the discussion at the next meeting that you attend? You will then become much more aware of the impact of non-verbal communication in your own interactions and negotiations. Expert communication in all its forms can make the difference between success and failure in any type of negotiation. Bear that in mind when you are next preparing to justify your budget proposals; even doing that provides a means of promoting the service. In justifying a new service, or the need for another member of staff, you also have the opportunity to put across a strong message about what the service is already doing. With careful preparation such messages can be transmitted extremely effectively.

PLANNING A CAMPAIGN

HOW TO PROMOTE

Having decided to promote the service the question is how? Each organisation will have its different emphasis and offer opportunities in different areas, for example business development or economic analysis and research, and therefore make certain approaches more appropriate than others. It is for you to choose, given your specific organisational climate.

As has been said, almost every interaction between information staff and others presents an opportunity to promote the service. The value of such opportunities should not be under-estimated. That is where the management style and leadership skills of the information manager will be reflected through the manner in which all information staff interact with users and potential users of the service. This makes a very important on-going contribution to the image of the service. Never forget that, unfortunate though it may be, one negative response or situation can often make the longest-lasting impression. Think of your users as customers who will keep you in business if the service is good.

However, customers will only come if they know about the service in the first place, so promotion cannot rely solely on the provision of a good service, which will be known only to those already interacting with the department. You need to get your message across outside the department. This may be in terms of one-off presentations or on-going promotions catering for the specialist needs of individuals and departments.

PRINTED MATERIAL

Ways of carrying out such promotion may involve the development of printed material, such as brochures, newsletters, bulletins, circulars. The reasons for issuing such publications are discussed by Kies who says that 'clarity of purpose is necessary if printed promotion pieces are to be used effectively.'[7]

In preparing these keep in mind the importance of good design and layout, house style and the possible use of a departmental logo. They must look professional, be effective, and the style and presentation constantly reviewed. Treat them like high quality press releases. Make them readable, clear and concise, putting across the desired corporate or departmental image. This also applies to SDI and current awareness services of all kinds. Examples of two promotional brochures are included in the appendix to *Marketing the modern information center*.[8]

PRESENTATIONS AND DEMONSTRATIONS

Talks, tours, and personal or group visits, all need to be well-structured and interesting. These may include departmental seminars, open-house sessions, presentations to particular groups or meetings, and induction programmes. In each case focus on what the service can do, rather than on the way in which it is organised. This applies to all presentations, in particular to induction sessions. First impressions really do count.

USE OF TECHNOLOGY

If you regularly access online databases or use various software programs, incorporate these into presentations wherever possible. They add another dimension, provide colour and, of equal importance, demonstrate yet another information skill.

PHYSICAL LAYOUT AND DISPLAY

The creation of the most effective visual impression requires just as much thought. If the service looks well-organised and attractive, it will be much more likely to be used. Details such as professional-looking, well-placed signs and labels plus the careful use of colour can also have considerable impact.

SERVICE REVIEW

To establish the best means of promotion a good starting point could be to conduct an information needs analysis. In the setting-up process you may already have carried this out. Therefore it would be a natural thing to make some kind of follow-up, possibly in the form of reviews of specific parts of the service, for example of the SDI. Even if you are not in the setting-up stage such reviews are vital and should certainly not be seen as one-off events.

Performance assessment and client surveys provide techniques through which to obtain feedback on services. They also offer valuable communication channels through which to interact with actual and potential clients. Reference to their use is made in *Personal development in information work*.[9]

Keeping yourself up to date is just as important as providing current awareness to clients — you cannot do one without the other. You need to keep up with developments relating to both the firm's interests and to library and information matters. Promotion is not just an internal activity. Make the service something that your organisation will regard as a positive asset, one which will give it the edge over competitors.

There is more to promotion than just publicising sources of information. The introduction of a new service, heightening the awareness of an existing one, emphasising any special staff skill or subject knowledge, are all part of the process. But before promoting any of these, you need to think of the possible consequences.

RESOURCING AND ORGANISING

Consider the total resourcing needed for each proposed promotion and ask yourself if you can satisfy the requirement. Do not undertake things which you cannot carry through. That will bring adverse publicity and could create long-term ill-will towards the department. Having said that, it could be that with some job-restructuring and increased use of information technology you could deliver those new services. Always consider the practical aspects, for example the time required to prepare talks, visual aids, brochures; to re-organise resources through improved labelling and signposting, stock review and replacement; the evaluation of new databases. All these are part of creating an enhanced and relevant service which you can further promote. It certainly underlines the importance of time management. Not only time taken, but the timing must be right. For example, if you want to make a presentation, check that nothing else of significance has been planned for that day by another department, and choose a theme of current interest to your selected audience.

Think about the administrative requirements in good time, co-ordinating the most suitable date for participants and booking the room in good time. Re-check both nearer the day. The most convenient time may be at lunch time or after office hours — if so organise some refreshments. Book any equipment and check that it is in working order. Nothing kills your professional image like the inability to start your presentation because the projector is not working. Remind yourself of the elements of good presentation, through some background reading or perhaps by attending a short course, preferably one which includes video-recording and feedback. The British Association for Commercial and Industrial Education (BACIE) booklet *Tips on talking*[10] provides a useful starting point, and BACIE also organises a three-day course on 'Effective presentations'.

THE BROADER ROLE

What has just been described is merely a summary of some of the tasks involved in preparing one promotional activity, but they are essential if it is to be a success. All promotional activities will require the same sort of careful thought and planning. Broader organisational involvement will give you higher visibility and show you to be capable of being active in areas not previously considered to be part of the librarian's role, for example records management, consultancy, client relations.

Alternatively, the role could be one of co-ordinating activities formerly carried out by several people in different departments, but which with creative direction could benefit the organisation and publicise not only the library *per se,* but also the range of skills of the library and information professional. For example, it may be appropriate for the information department to be the central point of contact for all external enquiries about the organisation's activities, as information staff are likely to be aware of the activities of most departments through the enquiry and current awareness processes.

Any broader role means more contact with people both inside and outside the organisation. Inside activities such as committee work present learning opportunities as well as the opportunity to contribute a view from a different set of work experiences and skills. For example, as a member of Stoy Hayward's Technical and Training Committee I was able to hear the accountant's viewpoint and put forward that of the information professional. This leads to greater understanding between the two disciplines and greatly assists service development. Outside activities provide another means of promoting your service and your organisation. Naturally this is something which you will have to agree with your employer, and which may require you to use your negotiating skills, in order for a satisfactory outcome to be reached. Activities such as lecturing and consultancy will cost the organisation in terms of staff time but may bring in revenue as well as publicity.

Both may generate spin-off, as the following example shows. When running an outside course, I mentioned that at Stoy Hayward we offered certain services externally on a fee-paying basis. Two days later one of my staff received a call asking for details of that service. We subsequently carried out several pieces of research for the company concerned. If you do offer services externally you may wish to produce a separate brochure describing what is an offer. This needs to be thought out in a different way to any document produced for internal use. What to include, what to omit, style, size, distribution, all need to be thought out with the particular target audience in mind.

Like anyone else in business you must be alert to opportunities. If you are approached by a potential client for general advice then try to see the whole spectrum across which you may be able to offer assistance. If consultancy is part of your role, then it is natural to offer such services, keeping in mind existing professional guidelines and codes of practice. When you have skills and resources which could help someone else, then why not make that fact known? It is good for you, for the department and for the firm. Outside activities, even attending a meeting or social event, give you the chance not only to promote your activities, but also to gain new insights and approaches, as well as to make new contacts.

Whatever form your promotion takes the most important thing about it is the overall approach. It should be seen as on-going and responsive to change, as should the service that you provide; it must be relevant to the organisation's needs and must always be timely. The whole essence of promotion is the constant seeking and identifying of opportunities, followed by the prompt implementation of ideas, i.e. turning thoughts into action whilst the need is still there. The state of mind required is one of constant awareness and alertness if such opportunities are to be realised. Successful promotion offers much beyond increased use of the service. It brings about considerable job satisfaction to the information professional and can further enhance the image and status of both the individual and the department, thereby assuring its continuing role as an essential central function of the organisation.

REFERENCES

1. SPECIAL LIBRARIES SECTION, LIBRARY ASSOCIATION OF AUSTRALIA, SOUTH AUSTRALIAN BRANCH. *Response to: SOUTH AUSTRALIA. Committee to review library services in South Australia. 'South Australian libraries, moving towards 2000'*. Adelaide: SA Government Printer, 1986. (RLSSA) .
2. PRYTHERCH, R. ed. *Staff training in libraries*. Aldershot: Gower, 1986.
3. WEBB, S.P. *Personal development in information work*. London: Aslib, 1986.
4. *Management Training Directory* 1988/89. 9th Edition. Reading: TFPL Publishing, 1988.
5. WOOD, M. S.   ed. *Cost analysis, cost recovery, marketing, and fee-based services. A guide for the Health Services librarian*. New York: Haworth Press inc., 1985.
6. INDUSTRIAL SOCIETY. *Guide to telephone techniques*. London: Industrial Society, 1986.
7. KIES, C. *Marketing and PR for libraries*. Metuchen NJ: Scarecrow Press, 1987.
8. SCHMIDT, J. *Marketing the modern information center: a guide to intrapreneurship for the information manager*. New York: FIND/SVP, 1987.
9. WEBB, S.P. *Personal development in information work*. London: Aslib, 1986.
10. BRITISH ASSOCIATION FOR COMMERCIAL AND INDUSTRIAL EDUCATION, *Tips on talking*. 2nd ed. London: BACIE, 1960.

CHAPTER FIVE
BUDGETING AND COSTING CAMPAIGN ACTIVITIES — PAYING THE PRICE AND VALUE FOR MONEY
Stephen A. Roberts

Conscious and purposive decisions to market and promote library and information services imply submission of those decisions to financial scrutiny. Marketing and promotion require resources. Value for money can never be assured, but risks can be minimized by planning those activities and ensuring that the financial aspects of the process are properly budgeted. Effective budgeting requires a knowledge of costs, and budgetary control is achieved by cost management and cost control. The 1980s have seen a greater regard for budgeting and costing aspects of library operations, although aspirations are often more substantial than achievements. In the past, marketing and promotion programmes were often (usually) regarded as little more than fringe activities, with a marginal claim on resources. Finance could and would be taken from a general administrative vote and the most significant recorded costs would be consumables (usually reprographic materials) and distribution costs. The assumptions underlying this chapter suggest a more developed and central role for marketing and promotion. Therefore, a larger claim on resources can be expected and this has to be justified financially.

The resource consequences of marketing and promotion need to be known by managers in greater detail and range. Marketing and promotion activities and costs cannot be hidden, and indeed should not be hidden in a marketing conscious organization. Other chapters have considered the purposes, aims, objectives and strategies of library campaigns — marketing planning, positioning, political aspects and promotional materials. The task of this chapter is to show the need for and principles of budgeting and costing approaches and awareness within the marketing and promotion campaign.

First of all some definitions of concepts are helpful. The general problem is one of resource management and resource allocation. Resources include *all* types of resources; material, human and intellectual, as well as financial. The managerial task is of resource management, both strategic and tactical; decision making with a strong financial element. Resource allocation is the central strategic concept. Put simply, how much of available resources is to be or needs to be committed in order to market and promote a product or service effectively?

A sense of financial orderliness would suggest a precise answer in terms of x per cent of resources; even in reality the strategic task is less clear cut, partly because the boundaries of the marketing task and the time-spending implications are fuzzy. To pin down some quantities is helpful, but pragmatically a realistic general overhead allocation may have to suffice. The general overhead then covers the time spent on meetings and communication (the creative input to marketing and promotion), market surveys, information collection and product development and evaluation (done in collaboration with the producers and technical specialists). As these tasks are performed the physical manifestations and consequences of them become clear and plannable; communication incurs telecommunications and direct transport costs; market surveys may require additional staff (incurring costs) and materials of various kinds.

The resource consumption and overhead burden of a marketing campaign bear some further analysis. When an organization is tackling a systematic campaign for the first time there is obviously very little experience and data to build on and give the manager a sense of confidence in the enterprise. A financial analysis of the effectiveness of the campaign is bound to come later and be retrospective. The first working budget may well be tentative and, frankly, hit and miss! The first attempt at resource allocation therefore needs very careful monitoring and checking as it proceeds, so that the different working stages and their progress can be meaningfully related to the final outputs, which may quite likely come after a substantial period of time. When campaigns can be repeated, the variance between budgeted costs and actual costs can be identified and sounder decisions taken by managers. A sounder knowledge of the overhead burden and associated costs does take time to acquire, and if this is to be with any precision there has to be some careful record keeping along the way of time spent on meetings (and who was involved in them) and the other tasks mentioned above.

An example can illustrate this. Using a technician to set up a display and providing documentation and materials for distribution has some strong elements of finite tasks, time spent and resultant costs. An external source may have been used to design and print materials, and competitive tendering may be the best way of establishing an appropriate level of costs. The differential costs of 1,000 or 10,000 leaflets or document packs will be evident. These elements of the operation are susceptible to monitoring, itemising and billing. The budget should identify these formally. These are variable costs which are determined by the overall scale of the operations.

On the other hand the overhead burden represents fixed costs; these have to be borne whatever the scale of the operation. The only thing variable about these fixed cost elements is their elastic nature — that is, there may be a very great deal of talking and other administrative input before anything tangibly productive is seen coming out from the campaign! The realization of this factor is crucial in appreciating the nature of overhead burden in managerial and administrative tasks. If a senior member of staff were to spend two days dealing with a promotional/marketing task, that may come close to one percentage point of their annual organizational cost. At a hypothetical cost of £30,000 per year that generates about £300 of overhead cost burden. Crude calculation though it is, it does give a figure which can be added to variable costs. The value of these kinds of expenditure to an organization depend in the long run on many other factors; the marketing effort for a competitively priced product with a suitably high unit price and strong demand can stand an appropriate level of cost.

Setting the level of resources for marketing and promotion in an organization is the key question and problem. The above discussion cannot answer the question for every organization, but it can stress some salient facts. Resources are needed to cover the direct and variable costs incurred; these can often be budgeted with some precision, since volume and other tangible aspects of the operation are known. Unless there is conscious and careful monitoring and intelligent use of past and accumulated experience the fixed cost burden of overheads can become startling and too high. Volume of demand and price can redeem the initial cost of promotion in the end and all may be well. But, there is a sharp lesson for management: marketing and promotion are in many instances geared to some kind of economic and commercial imperative. Where public sector organizations are essentially marketing and promoting public goods and welfare in a non-market, non-commercial situation there may be little to redeem a too high level of spend. The economics of marketing and promotion campaigns have then to be justified in political terms and policy goals, rather than in pure budgetary terms of cost and price.

The budget is the primary technique of organization for resource management, by virtue of its ability to display allocation to areas (programmes), and to sources of expense. The expenditure budget can be structured in line-item form (by headings of expense) or programme form (by areas of activity chosen according to organizational and operational need, which have identifiable financial/cost consequences).

In a marketing/promotion campaign the programme titles could be selected according to the functional sequence of operations. For example: planning and design (corresponding to a substantial proportion of the overhead burden); media and materials production; print and reprography; communication; distribution.

The manager can choose the programme areas which are helpful in identifying decisions, and monitoring and charting flows of resource consumption. Programme structured budgets are also known as performance budgets (e.g. as in the PPBS type — Planning, Programming Budgeting

System, because the systematic programme structure allows the manager to identify the resource allocation, consumption and output (performance) relationship). Performance budgets are considered to provide a better structure for assessing output measures and their direct financial and resource consequences. A good idea in principle, the practical realization can be variable and more administrative work is usually required. The method requires more effort and time to specify proposals and programmes and to chart the resource flows. In the first place the likely sequence of operations has to be modelled; considerable working detail may have to be grasped involving physical resources and task staffing. A budget manager cannot just concoct a paper plan and put this forward as a structure for the programmes; the procedure involves a distinctive empirical component.

Not all organizations can sustain such a level of budgetary planning and management. However, the pay-offs are significant — better knowledge of resource flows, better potential cost control, commitment to establishing definite outputs from resource allocations. As marketing and promotion activities achieve greater centrality, claim more resources and effort and require demonstrations of results, such a sophistication of resource management could be valuable and worthwhile. In practice a marketing/promotion spend of £1,000 or so may require little more than some line-item calculations of allocation and spending on a side of paper; but £10,000 or multiples thereof indicate a more sophisticated scale of budgeting, with a responsible manager and documentation to match. The bigger, and more costly, the marketing project the greater the scope for things to go wrong and for effectiveness and results to become dissipated. Many an expensive marketing/promotional campaign should have been halted, when it could have been ascertained (through cost and budget control) that it was not getting results. Campaigns that go on too long lose edge and may incur needless ineffective expenditure (look for stable sales and patronage patterns).

Costs represent sacrifices of resources, manifested as time spent and/or measured in monetary terms. Cost patterns are rarely absolute, and can be sensitive to the different ways of structuring, estimating, measuring and calculating them. Good practices and conventions can be offered, and whilst inter-organizational comparison may be problematic, cost calculation within organizations should be carried out under clear protocols and procedures to provide consistency. An extended discussion of cost study methods and implementation is provided in *Cost management for library and information services*.¹ Time study and time accounting aspects of costing should be carried out under explicit protocols known to all those involved. In most cases campaign managers will not be involved in such detailed costing, but they need to be aware of the protocols enforced if they are using secondary cost data derived from other studies. With experience working managers soon get a feel for costs, and procedural conscientiousness can form a guarantee that the data is 'clean'.

Campaign activities are sometimes diffuse and difficult to trace. Only a few key costs may be really essential and a pragmatic approach is to be recommended; the unit cost per item of promotional literature distributed or the costs of making a presentation to a client or group.

A macro or top-down approach will give the manager most of the data required to resolve the question of whether the original marketing decision was effective. The macro approach is synthetic rather than analytic; it requires a global view of the problem, a confident initial grasp of programme elements and resource needs, and the generation of key costs when results are being evaluated against performance standards and actual performance. Just as important are combined measures of cost and results (increase in sales revenue or patronage levels per input of promotion, e.g. after an exhibition or display event, or a round of visits to potential clients). These could be considered more formally as measures of cost/value and cost/benefit, although these are more difficult to generate. Marketing campaigns need identification in general organizational budgets, especially over a crucial size; expenditure needs estimating and recording; some knowledge of physical output is required and this will permit calculation of key unit costs. To summarize: how much is being spent on what; what levels of expense are necessary or tolerable, and what is the cost of the programme as a whole or for a part of it; these are the questions. Costing procedures and cost knowledge provide some of the answers.

Budgetary management of a campaign, from marketing planning to promotion, is really a type of system management. Input comes in the intellectual shaping of the campaign and in the physical use of resources. Intermediate outputs or throughputs can be identified, e.g. the production of media, exhibitions and displays. Then there are final outputs like the hours available for user/consumer contact, number of media packs distributed, as well as impacts and benefits as outputs from the system, albeit subjectively established. To what extent has the campaign increased turnover of patrons, documents or sales of a product or service (concrete items for the revenue side of the budget)? What benefits have been gained for the organization — greater visibility or increased market share?

It is at this stage that the question of value for money can be addressed. Was the campaign worthwhile; can its value or effect be demonstrated; can continued or greater campaign expense be justified? Should another approach be tried, or the present one abandoned or supplemented? In theory the systematic approach to resource management, budgeting and costing can help to answer these questions. The reality is, however, usually messier and a good deal more pragmatic. But there is a value to be gained from asking searching questions about the purpose, financing and resourcing of any marketing and promotion campaign at the outset. All this effort should be identified with the management information system of the organization. (Figure 1).

Figure 1 A SYSTEM FOR CAMPAIGN BUDGETARY MANAGEMENT

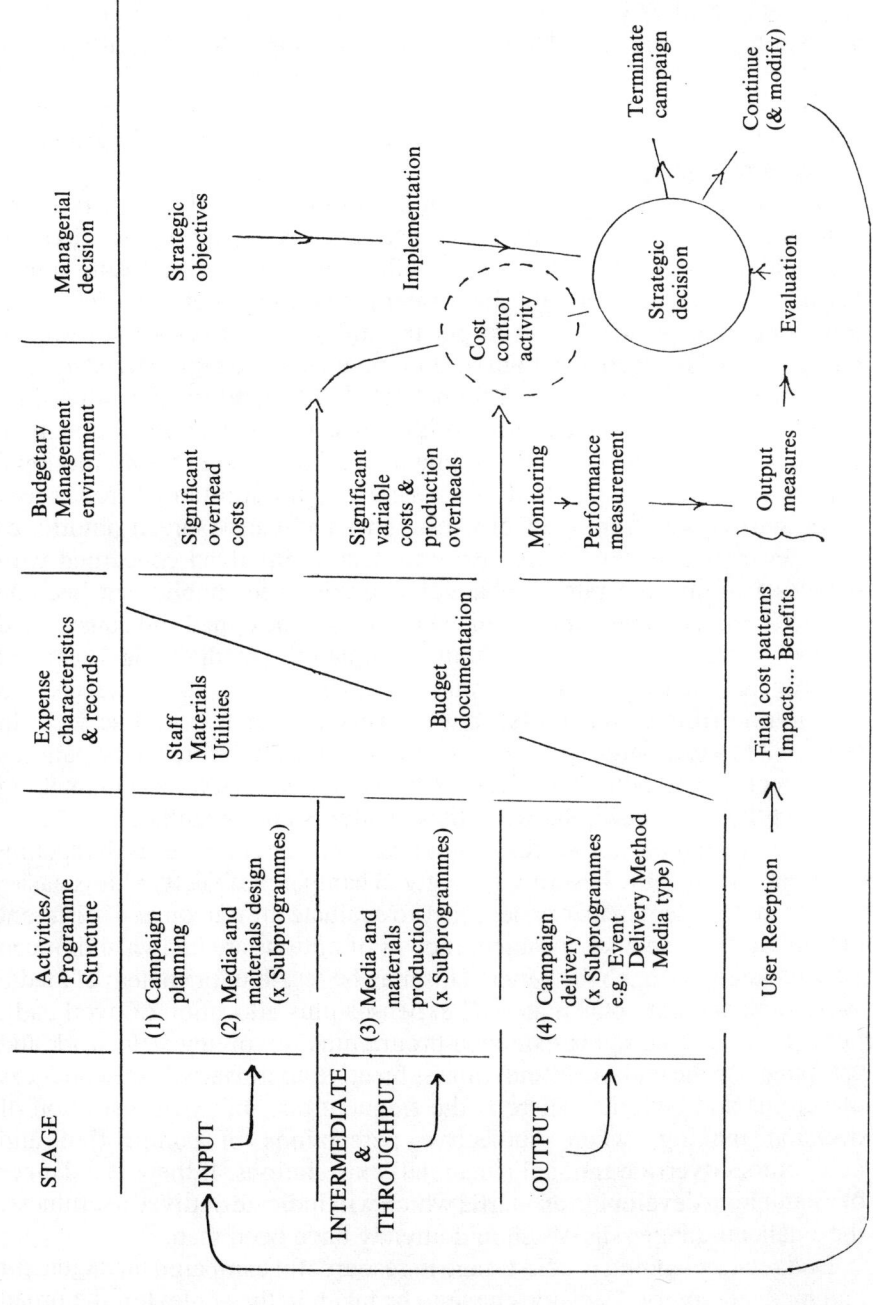

Should managing resources in general or a campaign in particular necessitate a knowledge of the character, extent and boundaries of the operations involved? The greater the control required, the more information required, even if the indicators produced such as unit costs are summative measures. A simple typology of campaign media that could be used to promote library and information activities can assist understanding and discussion (Figure 2).

Media campaigns are about the use and effects of different types of communication. At one end of the spectrum the interpersonal, direct or informal methods predominate; at the other, the medium of transmission is textual, material and formal. The former types need repetition often of an individual and personal kind to put the message across — the resource consequence is often one of high staff involvement and high staff costs. The latter types of 'media' have a higher 'shelf life' and greater durability. Leaflets can be produced from original design and artwork and then duplicated at marginal cost, according to level of demand for promotional activity. Static displays and exhibitions may require substantial preparatory work, and may represent a capital investment which can be spread (amortised) over several years. There are also time factors involved concerned with obsolesence and the rate of change. The consumer public can become 'bored' with the same gimmick or even carefully designed and constructed display. Organizational needs change, but can the media budget respond flexibly and rapidly? More formal methods can be staff intensive in preparation (direct staff costs), but delivery can be user self-service. In many cases a campaign will use a mix of media, with different cost patterns and effectiveness potentials. The substance of budgetary decision making is about the relationship between these patterns and potentials.

This immediately introduces a complexity into the resource and budgeting problem. What is the best mix for a given campaign objective? It is easier to state the problem in theory; less easy to evaluate the outcomes of different options and decide upon a choice. If costs of options are known and/or can be calculated, so much the better. This may be feasible for an item of media (staff time and cost plus materials expenses plus allocation of overhead), but less so for a complex extended programme, involving field work and campaigns in the real world and some subjective appraisals of consequences of actions and benefits. There is the frequent possibility of distortion of decision making, where subjective perceptions of competition and competitors override rational (financial) expectations. If there is a danger of a campaign developing an inertia which will indicate outlived usefulness, the financial danger signals should already have been read.

Budgetary planning is a first stage in resourceful campaign management and media delivery. Decisions have to be taken in the context of the broad range of methods and resource consequences. The reasons for constructing

Figure 2 SIMPLIFIED TYPOLOGY OF CAMPAIGN MEDIA

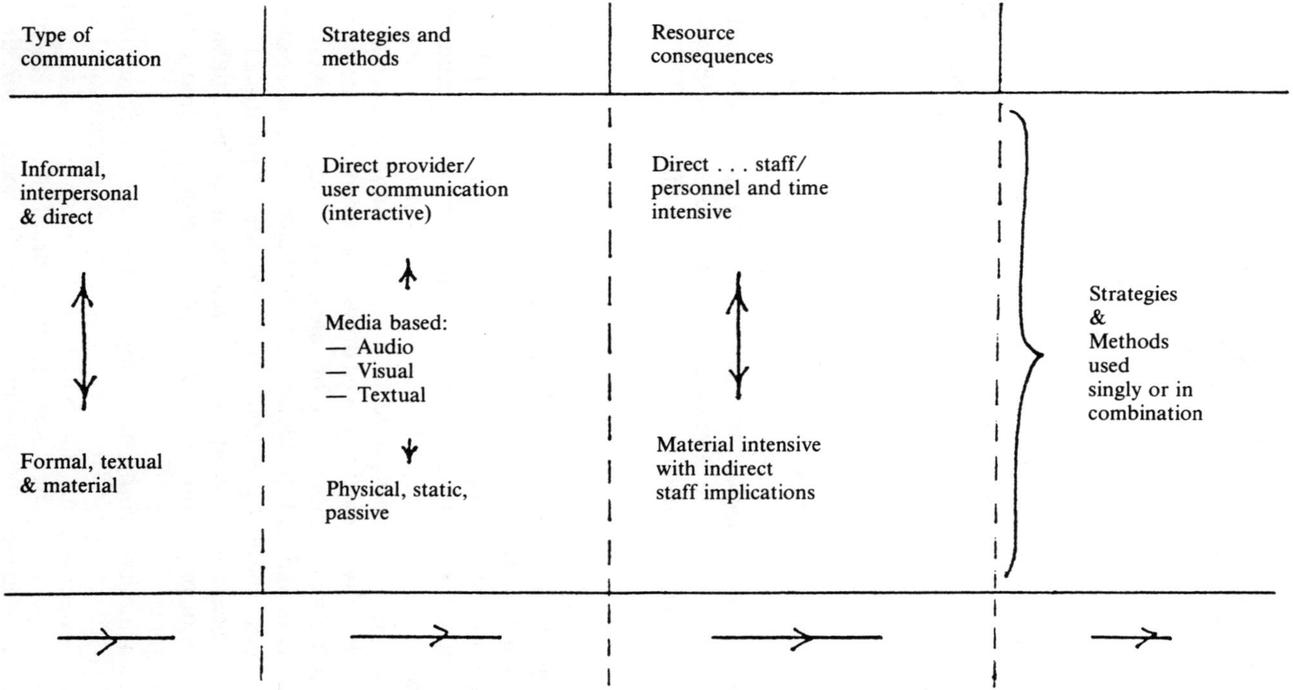

Type of communication	Strategies and methods	Resource consequences	
Informal, interpersonal & direct	Direct provider/ user communication (interactive)	Direct... staff/ personnel and time intensive	Strategies & Methods used singly or in combination
	Media based: — Audio — Visual — Textual		
Formal, textual & material	Physical, static, passive	Material intensive with indirect staff implications	

53

a campaign budget and deriving particular resource allocations have a better chance of being understood. The outcomes of the campaign should be more successful, at least as far as media and promotion effort are concerned. It also becomes possible to separate out controllable effects from those consequent on faulty strategic decision making. A misunderstanding of the market and production of an inferior product can be diagnosed as such and not blamed on deficiencies of promotion. Promotion is really a vehicle; you get the media you are prepared to pay for in your campaign, and should look elsewhere for explanations of success or failure. This is not to say that good promotional campaigns are not responsible for success or for failure; you can have successful promotion of a poor product as well as poor promotion of a good product. But there may be other causes, and it is these that need to be known. Such an excursion into diagnosis and analysis is important at the review phase of the budget. Will we repeat the past experience or try a new strategy or method? Budgeting is an ongoing repeating process, which is part of the critical review of managerial and organizational performance.

The essential questions then in resourcing a campaign stem from these considerations: fail to appreciate and understand these and you may experience a failure in understanding the statistical costs. The key questions are:

how much (money and resources — already in stock or paid for) to achieve certain objectives (sales, turnover, market share, information transfer, message communication)

by what methods and media (the appropriate mix)

for how long (the optimum plan and campaign period)?

An end dimension is knowing when to stop — campaigns are liable to diminishing returns (the piles of undistributed expensively produced leaflets!) Also, when the success curve has begun the campaign needs may change and media delivery can be slowed down to a minimum necessary to achieve a desired effect (maintenance of sales, usage etc). The production of the media campaign and its apparatus must be cost-effective, give value for money and benefits to the consumer (accurate information, meeting needs and demands) and to the supplier (increase market share, stable or reducing unit costs of production and promotion, relative position with respect to competitors).

A clear understanding of strategy and a clear budgetary statement are essential first stages. This need not demand sophisticated or complex budget documentation; the budget is as much a working concept and hypothesis as a statistical statement and proof of achievement. Value for money is obtained by producing what is needed for the campaign economically: this is an internal organizational matter which rests upon good management and effective technology and techniques and a skilled and competent workforce.

Can you deliver what you need for the campaign, without sacrificing other organizational needs? This is no small question for the one-or few-person bands which are the norm in the information providing world. Do not budget to do a job in-house which is going to be beyond reasonable capability. The public reception of media is fickle and subjective, and we cannot argue with a taste that is attuned to a good deal of gloss. The ideal for most organizations may be an economical professionalism, which gives an effective and economic result with some aesthetic value (if it is media based) or honest impact without the need for costly deception. It is better to spend a bit more using a contractor or consultant and thus guarantee results. You can always sue defaulting suppliers, even if this incurs additional cost.

The more significant the campaign to the organization and the greater its resource consequences, the firmer the reason for preparing a formal budget statement (usually as a detailed annexe to any mainstream budgetary documentation). Printing some publicity leaflets for direct distribution may require no more than a note of how much paper is needed or was used and the use charges for photocopying. But even this case can benefit from a knowledge of how much staff time went into developing a concept for the brochure and discussion; marketing and promotion have their opportunity costs too. All these factors contribute to the real cost of the publicity and the promotion. In many cases the questions are more likely to be asked after the event! So much better to do it before! Whatever, the data should be recorded; the costs (staff time and materials and overhead costs) can help to inform future budgeting.

A more elaborate campaign can be envisaged, such as one to promote a new branch library, and would require different media for adequate publicity. For example, a poster campaign, leafleting to households, advertising in the local press, a press day before the event (with hospitality expenses), a launch/opening on the great day (with extra exposure from local TV and radio), and then internal promotional materials to facilitate use and exploitation of the new library. Similar exercises could be envisaged in different types of library, information service or in an organization (where the objective is to promote some aspect of information and communication). Some typical elements that have to be considered can be exemplified in the stages of a scenario reflecting campaign programme areas.

1. *Campaign planning*

This should establish the concept of the campaign, lines of action, means of delivery and sources, and responsibilities for organization and production. All these are managerial tasks which lay out some of the future cost patterns. This programme carries a substantial share of fixed (overhead) costs. Staff time (and costs reflected in those staff) is the main budget item. On the first time round this is difficult to estimate since discussion of the campaign is not always confined to visible, formal communication. In a large organization a middle manager should assume overall line responsibility for the campaign and gain some control over time spent and involvement (hence controlling overheads).

2. Media and materials design

Campaign needs can be isolated and design tasks allocated. This will normally be the work of technical specialists, and may be done in-house or externally. The design stage should include the material costs of any prototypes and mock-ups. Materials costs can be estimated on an historical basis, from recent invoices or from supplier estimates. One trap to avoid here is to make insufficient allowance for inflation. If the work is done in-house staff times need to be monitored and recorded. An allowance is needed for organizational overhead costs (building, services, utilities). Overhead costs can be rated on a staff grade basis or a percentage factor applied to a job: generous overhead allowances do give a margin for comfort, and variances can be adjusted at the end of the budget period.

3. Media and materials production

Different media have to be distinguished and allowed for in specific production and cost packages (sub-programmes). Staff costs and materials will be the two principal expense categories, supplemented by production overheads and a general overhead apportioned from the planning and design stage (stages 1 and 2 above).

4. Campaign delivery

Running various promotional events and distribution of publicity material should be seen as a specific budgetary programme. Once again staff time may be the main source of expense, but there will also be materials and equipment expenditure (e.g. catering, petty cash incidentals) and communication expenditure (e.g. transport, postage, telephones). Once the initial launch has been accomplished the ongoing costs of keeping the campaign visible could be subsumed in this programme (e.g. replenishment of promotional materials), with an appropriate adjustment to the materials production cost.

These four broad programme areas provide a useful foundation for campaign budgeting and programme management. Experience will lead to embellishment and refinement. At the end the campaign will have to be evaluated; this could involve meetings and surveys, and the costs could be added to programme. The most important aspect is to have a means whereby the manager can reasonably account for all expenditures and costs. Total costs can provide the basis for calculating unit costs, and variable costs can be distinguished from fixed costs (overheads). Units of output have to be distinguished, and this may not be easy to do; units may vary between a total event, an item of media or some less tangible communication event. The evaluation may have to be delayed until the use or sales curves associated with the campaign change shape, providing an aggregate measure of output.

To summarize and conclude, one could begin by observing that much that has been written here is merely good sense or a triumph of expectation over practice. Costing is an imperfect art at the best of times; even statistical perfection does not always attain the truth as far as it relates to organizational economics. This chapter has tried to clarify a position. It starts with the view that marketing and promotion have been marginal activities in library services, especially as regards managerial and budgetary practices, until the professional upsurge of interest in the theme in the late 1970s. Now, under the influence of resource cuts, a critical evaluation of service and product philosophy, and burgeoning enterprise and market driven influences the theme and its activities is fast becoming central. Commercially orientated library and information services will do themselves little justice and a lot of harm if they do not identify marketing and promotion amongst their major economic programmes. To cope with this emerging situation and its managerial and economic realities will require a combination of good sense, understanding of some economic and budget theory and enhanced practices in resource allocation and management. There is now a severely reduced margin for error in managing and running library campaigns, which will tend to become more ambitious in line with market conditions and subject to greater cost scrutiny — in fact more than ever like other areas of library operation such as collection development and technical services.

Perhaps unfortunately, this chapter cannot be prescriptive for every individual need in running a campaign from a budgetary and cost angle. However, in most cases the quality of background thinking is a real determinant of the economic health of a library campaign. A step-by-step analysis of the problem and the options is necessary; this chapter has highlighted some of the questions and considerations.

Initially, the resources needed for the campaign should be listed, in accordance with the tasks they contribute to and the staff involved in realization. Price and cost tags can then be assigned. This information will be shaped to the organization's budgetary practices and absorbed within it. This is fine for those organizations operating within this framework. Many small library and information organizations lack the framework, but the initial analysis mentioned above will go a long way as an interim measure. The analysis of options also requires an analysis of outcomes expected; if revenue yields or patronage increases can be quantified at that point, the direction of cost-effectiveness and cost-value of the campaign can be detected. Actual costing procedures and budgetary methods are in reality more complex and time consuming; Alley and Cargill[2] Roberts,[1] and Smith[3] give further detail on costing and accounting; Koenig and Stam[4] offers a broader perspective of budgeting which could be valuable for the larger organizational canvas. The collection of papers edited by Cronin[5] is still valuable for inspirational reading, but every practitioner will bear in mind that the literature on finance and marketing in business is large, growing and often less than helpful to the needs and interpretations required in the information and library field. With these directions and cautions in mind intending campaign managers should not stray too far off the financial track.

REFERENCES

1. ROBERTS, S.A. *Cost management for library and information services.* London: Butterworths, 1985.
2. ALLEY, B. *and* CARGILL, J. *Keeping track of what you spend: the librarian's guide to simple bookkeeping.* Phoenix: Oryx Press, 1982.
3. SMITH, G.S. *Accounting for librarians and other not-for-profit managers.* Chicago: American Library Association, 1983.
4. KOENIG, M.E.D. *and* STAM, D.C. Budgeting and financial planning for libraries. *In: Advances in Library Administration and Organization,* 4, 1986.
5. CRONIN, B. *ed. The marketing of library and information services.* London: Aslib, 1981. (Aslib Reader Series, volume 4).

CHAPTER SIX
POLITICAL LOBBYING
George Cunningham

Some members of the library and information profession might wonder why anyone in the profession should want to go in for the business of political lobbying. Surely, they might say, we are above that nasty business. I would just ask them to recall the birth of the public library movement in the United Kingdom. It was born on the floor of the House of Commons when Members of Parliament like William Ewart, by their irritating persistence, forced less perceptive colleagues to recognise the case for the modest legislation of 1850. They had to argue against people like Colonel Charles Sibthorp, the Member for Lincoln, who said he had never liked reading even when he was at Oxford and that demands for free Punch and Judy shows would follow if you once conceded free libraries.

Today it is not only public libraries that are threatened by decisions taken in Whitehall and Westminster. University and college library services are just as affected by funding decisions taken in the political world. School library services stand to suffer by arrangements made by ministers and MPs about the institutional framework in which schools are managed. Business interests too, requiring ready access to information in order to compete in the modern world, stand to gain or lose by the decisions taken by politicians on the extent of information services provided to the public and the policy adopted on charging for them.

It is no longer only political decisions by our own British government which affect the profession and the service. Increasingly, the European Community is taking initiatives in this field. Networking between European libraries, and the possible creation of a grandiose 'European Library' are just two recent examples of Community ideas. Taxes on books and other information vehicles, copyright law, the control of book prices — these are only the first of subjects closely affecting the profession on which we shall be governed by law made not in Westminster but in Brussels.

If organisations and individuals who speak for the library and information services do not know how to affect political decisions they will have to endure what they cannot prevent. But the business of making representation in political quarters is not an easy one. The corridors of Whitehall,

Westminster and Brussels are familiar enough to those of us who have trodden them; but to most people they are as forbidding and unknown a territory as King Minos's labyrinth, and their successful negotiation as unlikely. As a general rule, those who have no experience in this field are ill advised to take it on themselves. That is why we have seen the burgeoning of so many public relations and parliamentary consultants, many of whom are not much less blind than their clients. Reliable advisers are hard to find and they do not come cheap. People and organisations in the Library Association's extended family would do well to turn in the first instance to us at Head Office who have experience under our belt and some successes to our credit.

Perhaps the best way to convey an idea of the problems and the means of overcoming them is to take a recent campaign — that to prevent the British government imposing VAT on books and other forms of literature in 1984 and 1985. Two years later a new campaign on the same matter had to be mounted to resist the same threat, coming this time from the European Commission. As I write, the outcome of this second chapter is uncertain but we do know that the earlier operation succeeded. How did we do it and what lessons can we learn from that experience?

It was in the late Spring of 1984 that we started getting information that the government was examining the case for applying VAT to books, journals, newspapers and magazines. Publishers, booksellers and authors had most to lose financially from the proposal but the Library Association was as fiercely opposed as the associations representing those interests. Local authorities would be able to recover VAT paid on books bought by public and school libraries but there would be a costly administrative effort involved in the process and university libraries, to take just one example, would not be entitled to recover the tax. The various associations therefore formed a committee, under the *aegis* of the National Book Committee, and under the chairmanship of Viscount Macmillan, now the Earl of Stockton, President of the Publishers' Association — and not unfamiliar with the corridors of power. Money was raised to produce leaflets, posters and background briefs. Since none of our organisations could undertake the work involved from normal staff a firm of consultants was commissioned to do the hard graft of contacting civil servants, members of both Houses of Parliament and, of course, ministers.

But first a tactical issue had to be settled. Some ministers who claimed to be sympathetic to our aims suggested that the campaign committee should lie low for a while, preparing its briefing papers but not going high profile. Better, they said, to rely on making serious representations to government about the economic effects of VAT on books shortly before the Budget statement. That would be more likely to succeed than stirring up a lot of MPs to bombard government with letters and parliamentary questions which would only put up the backs of both ministers and officials. That was a judgment which I strongly rejected. There are times when the 'softly softly' approach is right; but this was not one of them. The British government was under no strong pressure from Brussels or elsewhere to make the change. The economic case on our side was real, but there was a case on the other side which government was likely to find more appealing. What we had to do was brutally simple: to get across to ministers that if they set about imposing VAT they would run into more trouble from their own back-bench MPs than the business was worth. Persuading the government that the issue was a hot one and that they might only burn their fingers on it was the task.

On operations like this, you must take your chances when you can. I was due to speak at the annual dinner of the Library Committee of the City of London Corporation on July 10th and used the occasion to warn the government that if they went ahead with the idea they would encounter the united opposition of all who cared for literary culture, including the thousands of library users in the constituencies of the government's own MPs. The government had just recently had to back down on another proposal because of opposition in its own ranks. The concluding advice to the Chancellor of the Exchequer was to forget about VAT on books because, we promised, if he did not he would get another bloody nose. Some of the City Corporation representatives present thought the speech went over the top: that was the intention and it succeeded in pushing the issue out into the open. A leading article in the *Daily Telegraph* picked up the speech and advised the government to think again.

That autumn the campaign targeted ministers, civil servants and, above all, those Conservative back-bench MPs whom we judged to be open to persuasion. The case was a combination of detailed economic argument and an appeal to that old watchword 'no tax on knowledge'. 'No tax on reading', we said and got that message across by mass distribution of leaflets and petition forms, organised in bookshops by the Booksellers' Association and in libraries by the Library Association. The Consumers' Association did tremendous work through the medium of its mass circulation magazine *Which*. The Consumers' Association and the Library Association ended up presenting thousands of petition forms at the door of 10 Downing Street one windy morning in February.

''Tis not in mortals to command success, But we'll do more Sempronius; we'll deserve it'. So said Addison in *Cato*. Certainly the hundreds of people who put time into this campaign deserved success and on this occasion we got it. When the Chancellor of the Exchequer delivered his Budget speech in March, he said he would not put VAT on books either then or for the rest of the Parliament. He went on to say he had never thought of doing so but we had our sources inside government and we knew otherwise. The campaign was a good illustration of fitting the methods to the situation and exercising effective pressure at the critical point.

By contrast, consider the effort mounted by the Library Association in 1985 to persuade the British Government not to withdraw from UNESCO, the United Nations Educational Scientific and Cultural Organisation. Britain had been one of the founders of UNESCO after the war, but felt, along with the United States, that the Organisation had become too political and that its Senegalese Director General, Mr. M'Bow, was wasting its resources on inefficient administration and pet projects harmful to the West. The United States had withdrawn its membership the year before and Britain had now given notice that it would do the same. In the Library Association we felt that, whatever criticisms might be made of some aspects of the administration of UNESCO, its operations on library matters were free of them and of value to countries in the Third World. How could we best influence the government's final decision?

There was little chance of stirring up mass protests on such an issue. The press, insofar as it covered the issue at all, came down in favour of withdrawal. The Prime Minister, we knew, had little sympathy with those who wanted to stay in. But there were other ministers, at lower level, who thought we should stay in and fight for reform from within. We judged that the best weapon to hand was the Select Committee on Foreign Affairs, one of the permanent committees of the House of Commons charged with watching over a government department, in this case the Foreign Office, and the area of policy it covers. Members of that committee were approached. We said it would be curious indeed if Britain were to leave the organisation it had done so much to create without the Committee addressing its mind to the issue and giving its opinion to the government. The Committee, like others of its kind, had plenty of other issues on its plate but the members agreed that they should make a quick examination of the issue. At short notice the Library Association was invited to present its views to the Committee. In July 1985 the Association's representatives spent an hour making its case to the Committee. We made sure that we were represented by people whom the Committee would recognise as having valuable experience in the field. The group included Sir Harry Hookway, former Chief Executive of the British Library and President of the Association, and Max Broome, active over many years in IFLA and for the British Council. Horses for courses is the rule on such occasions.

When the Committee produced its report we were delighted that they came down in favour of staying in UNESCO. With this behind us, some argued that we should now go high profile and stir up as much noise as we could. We decided not to do so. If the decision were taken below prime ministerial level we had a good chance of success. If it were taken at Number 10, we had little. 'Keep low' was our watchword. But of course there were others engaged in this battle, people who knew the ground rules as well as we did but with different objectives. In the event the issue did get decided at top level and, despite a debate in the House of Commons where not a single Member supported withdrawal, the government announced that Britain would leave UNESCO at the end of the year. We had done all we could, using a quite different set of spanners than those we used on VAT, but this time, Sempronius, we did not command success.

These two issues were ones where legislation was not involved. For the most part however those trying to influence political decisions are trying to kill or amend a bill going through Parliament, or of course to push a bill through. In the parliamentary session 1987/88 the Library Association had a strong interest in the Copyright Bill, the Education Bill and two Local Government Bills. In cases like these the processes are different, and a close knowledge of parliamentary procedure is needed.

Normally, a bill starts in the House of Commons. It is 'read a first time' as a pure formality, meaning only that the text is printed. A day is then set aside for its 'second reading'. This is the main debate on the general principles of the bill and at the end of the debate a vote is taken. It is rare indeed for bills put forward by the government, which means the vast majority of bills, to fall at this hurdle, rare even for an MP not to vote with his own side. The bill is then sent to a committee for detailed consideration. In the case of a very important measure the committee might be a committee of the whole House, in which all MPs can take part. Otherwise the committee is made up of anything from 16 to 35 Members, the ratio between parties reflecting as nearly as possible the make-up of the House itself. The committee goes through the bill line by line, considering amendments by Members and either passing them or killing them. In such committees Members are rather more willing to do what they should do all the time — think before they vote and then vote the way they think. It is not therefore a hopeless task to get an amendment carried against the wishes of the government in a committee. This committee stage may last anything from one sitting for a tiny uncontroversial bill to dozens of sittings for a big and controversial one. Sittings normally last two and a half hours a week. At the end, the bill, amended according to the decisions of the committee, is sent back to the House as a whole. It is then subject to a 'Report stage' normally lasting one day during which any Member can propose further amendments. However, because of shortage of time, the Chair has great discretion in selecting amendments for consideration at this stage and many a Member finds himself unable to get his amendment put to the vote, far less debated. A 'Third reading' debate then takes place (so long as a handful of Members want it) and a final vote is taken on whether the bill, now in its final form, should be passed.

If it is passed, the bill then goes to the House of Lords where it undergoes the same process except that in the Lords the committee is always a committee of the whole House. In order to lessen congestion in the House of Lords at the end of the session, some bills start in the Lords and go on to the Commons. If the two Houses have passed the identical text the bill receives the Royal Assent and becomes law. If the two Houses disagree, the bill must pass back and forth between the two until one House gives in. Normally the House of Lords knows its place and backs down but shortage of parliamentary time will often lead the government to compromise in the face of strong opposition in the Lords.

Organisations endeavouring to influence the texts of bills must provide briefs to sympathetic MPs and peers and if they have any sense they will make that word 'brief' earn its name. Parliamentarians may not all be wildly busy but they do not take kindly to thirty-page documents on complex issues, nor to self-styled experts who cannot express themselves lucidly in a simple manner. The best advice is — identify the points which matter most to your organisation and on which there is some chance of success; forget the rest. Next — pick your man or woman with care. Some MPs and peers could not argue themselves out of a paper bag; leave them alone. Go for people with a record not only of making a point but of getting others to accept it.

There are other mechanisms for making points in Parliament besides the passage of legislation. Every day, Ministers answer Members' questions. If it is simply information you want, questions can be tabled for written reply, provided the information is relevant to the Minister's functions. If the intention is to advertise an issue the Member will go for an oral question, giving him both greater exposure and the chance to put a supplementary question after the initial question has been answered. Then there is the device of the adjournment debate when a Member (if he is lucky in a ballot) can mount a case to a Minister over fifteen minutes at the close of the day's sitting with the Minister having the same time to reply. No decision is taken and 'debate' is a misnomer since only the one Member and the Minister take part, but the adjournment debate, skilfully used, is a valuable arrow in the intelligent Member's quiver.

So far I have dwelt exclusively on activities in Parliament because that is a field about which outsiders are most in the dark. However, any campaign directed at national decision takers must also use the press, radio and television if it is to create a sympathetic background against which governmental or parliamentary decisions are taken.

It is notoriously difficult to get media coverage for complex issues. You may think your cause is worthy of front page headlines but the chances are that the editors and journalists will not. You have to be prepared to invest a lot of time and trouble for little result. In this field there is everything to be gained from personal contact. A journalist with whom you maintain regular contact can guide you on what news stories stand a chance of getting into print. Besides news cover, do not overlook the possibilities of a feature article. Here again, informal contact with journalists will help.

Getting exposure on national radio and television is the most difficult. You should remember that there are now hundreds of local radio stations hungry for stories. They want material that has a local relevance and it's up to you to satisfy them that there is a story there that the public will want to hear about.

When issuing press releases make it snappy. Put the best bit at the beginning, don't make it too long and type it double-spaced on one side of each sheet. Be sure to give a phone number for whoever can answer queries.

Campaigns should also target local organisations and MPs in their localities. There can be no doubt that Members of Parliament pay more attention to representations made by residents in their constituencies than to those made by national organisations; for the very good reason of course that local residents have votes. Let no one pour scorn on this sensitivity of the MP to his local constituents; the vote exists exactly to foster such responsiveness to the people the MP represents.

Most MPs these days are assiduous in replying to letters from constituents. The time when an MP simply passed letters from constituents to the relevant Minister under cover of a standard form and then passed the Minister's comments back to the constituent under another are gone. So are the days when Members had to pay for 'phone calls and stamps from their own pocket and had no allowance to pay for a secretary. Have no hesitation therefore in getting in touch with your own MP and insist on a proper reply. Remember that MPs are parochial in their attitude to territory. Don't contact the MP next door just because you think he's more likely to be sympathetic. The protocol of Parliament stops one MP interfering in another's constituency.

If you are organising a campaign and getting lots of people to write to the same Member, don't treat him like a donkey. Aim for his head, not his backside. Don't get hundreds of people to write identical letters from a text you have supplied. Much better to spend time drawing up a brief which sets out the case clearly, but as simply as possible. Make clear what you are asking the Member to do. That brief can then be used by lots of people who can send it to the Member under cover of a letter which each has prepared himself.

By all means ask to have a meeting with the MP. Most Members make themselves available to constituents on set days in the month. If the meeting you want is likely to need more than ten minutes, better to write and ask for a special appointment. It's hard for a Member to concentrate on your notions of the law of copyright in between listening to Mrs. Smith's complaint on social security and Mr. Brown's on a leaking roof. Don't feel that you need to go and see the Member at the House of Commons. It's nice for you to have a day out in London but the MP is not just sitting there twiddling his thumbs waiting for constituents to arrive to discuss something that could have been more sensibly discussed in his constituency. As for mass lobbies with groups from all over the country converging on the Commons to nobble their MPs all on the same day, that practice is a silly one, only justified when the objective is to create a visible peg for media publicity. The effect is nearly always less satisfactory than that which can be achieved by a quiet and relaxed meeting at an agreed time.

I said earlier that more and more issues in the library and information services field are affected by the doings of the European Community. Even the task of finding out what is going on inside that massive structure is a formidable one. The main institutions of the Community are:

The European Commission. This is the civil service of the Community, staffed by people drawn from all twelve member states, based mainly in Brussels.

The European Parliament. Since 1979 the Parliament comprises members elected every five years directly by the public. Britain has 81 Members of the European Parliament (MEPs) each representing an area the size of eight or nine normal British constituencies. The Parliament meets in full session once a month in Strasbourg. In the intervening weeks the many committees of the Parliament meet, normally in Brussels.

The Council of Ministers. This comprises ministers from member states. The law of the community, which prevails over the domestic law of member states, is made by the Council of Ministers and not by the Parliament but the Parliament has a growing influence on the process of Community law making.

Although the British public has hardly got used to the fact that there are such things as European Members of Parliament for each bit of the country, it is important to use them on matters being considered in the Community. Local libraries can provide the addresses where MEPs can be contacted and many of them hold 'surgeries' for constituents to raise matters just as in the case of MPs. Because the European Parliament has no one site it is not normally sensible to try to contact MEPs when they are at their meetings. Better to use the local address and, if a meeting is needed, arrange one during the Member's time in his constituency.

Sometimes the issue on which representations are to be made are in the control not of national government but of the local authority. On such cases should one deal only with local councillors and leave the MP out of it? There are still some MPs who will not touch an issue which properly belongs to the local authority. But they are few and getting fewer. Most MPs will make representations to local councils and many are much better at doing it than local councillors. So by all means try the MP. He will at least advise you on how you can best go about the task.

When you are dealing with councillors on local authorities, however, remember that, just as MPs take a particular interest in their own constituencies, councillors are concerned with the area they represent. Find out which ward or other electoral district is affected by your cause and which councillors represent it. Then find out which of the committees of the council are concerned with the matter and go for the members of those committees, irrespective of the areas they represent. If you can manage it, get local residents in a councillor's own ward to put the case.

Although it is worthwhile to get MPs active on local issues, it rarely helps to get councillors trying to affect national issues. An exception to that rule is when you can get the council as a whole to make representations to government or to its MPs. Many councils have succeeded in sensitising their local MPs to issues like VAT on books by means of letters explaining how much more cost and administrative bother would be entailed in a change in legislation. Councils can also be got to raise matters of general concern with the various local authority associations — the Association of County Councils, the Association of Metropolitan Authorities, etc.

The golden rule is that you should bring pressure to bear at as many points as possible. Do not try to be too tidy. Better for your targets to receive large numbers of letters saying not quite the same thing than to receive a few in identical terms. Let a thousand blunderbusses bloom!

Finally, remember that what you want is results. If the MP shows you his speech in the House in which he put your point, ask yourself, and ask him 'Yes, but did you achieve what we wanted?' Of course you cannot expect one Member to win against a hostile House of Commons. But don't be too easily satisfied with words. It's results that count.

CHAPTER SEVEN
EDUCATING STAFF FOR PUBLIC RELATIONS
Darlene E. Weingand

Within this volume of approaches to PR campaigns, there is a need for reflection on the relationship between public relations and the initial educational preparation of library professional personnel. The importance of including educational content at this pre-service level cannot be overemphasized, for it is here that the foundation in knowledge, skills and attitudes is either firmly laid – or neglected. As a component of the entire foundation of library science, the string of concepts that link the library with its community on many levels is core to developing a mindset that is proactive and able to deal effectively with a changing society.

Although this chapter focuses on initial pre-service preparation, it would be remiss not to stress at the outset that pre-service education is but the beginning of a continuum of education that stretches throughout a career. Once the library science degree is in hand, it serves as a key to further continuing education experiences that will keep the new graduate competent and current throughout his or her professional lifetime. With this mental image of a continuum in mind, it is then time to focus on educational beginnings.

COMMUNICATION: THE BASELINE

Public relations can best be regarded as a system of *communication*. In the standard communication model, there is a sender, a message which is encoded and transmitted through a channel of communication, and a receiver who decodes the message and, hopefully, provides feedback to the sender. The channel of communication may be interpersonal or mediated, depending on the nature of the message. It is important to remember that, throughout the process, individual dissonance based on the receiver's own level of attention and experience will create barriers to clear understanding. Therefore, the feedback loop is essential to the process if the accuracy of transmission is to be ascertained. In interpersonal communication, this loop may be created quite naturally; in mass communication, or broadcast communication, securing feedback is a much more difficult endeavour.

Why is this brief discussion of the communication model important? Nitecki states that:

> to accomplish their primary function of linking users to needed information, public services librarians must master various skills ... (i) to communicate with others, (ii) to analyse needs (iii) to retrieve data, (iv) to instruct users, and (v) to manage operations and supervise staff who provide services.[1]

In each example, the skill is rooted in some form of communication, with communication itself at the top of the list.

However, in typical initial professional education, little attention is directed toward the process, opportunities and problems which govern communication. Most coursework is knowledge or skill-based, specifically oriented towards library-specific tasks and activities. The whole notion of communication as an essential skill, even if articulated in the curriculum, is often passed over lightly. This pattern may be shifting as library schools move toward changing both departmental names and curricula to reflect the importance of information in the library's mission. In addition, there is an emerging trend (Rutgers University in the United States as one example) towards combining departments; library studies with such disciplines as communication, computer science and information science. These institutional movements may well herald an acknowledgement of the significance of communication as a core element in contemporary librarianship.

THE ELEMENTS OF PUBLIC RELATIONS

If communication is truly the baseline, how then can public relations be defined and how can public relations be adequately dealt with in a pre-service curriculum?

Kies states that 'Contemporary definitions of public relations stress its reliance upon two-way communication and its role as a management responsibility'.[2] This placement of public relations as a component of the managerial role is a critical one. It raises the relative importance of public relations efforts to a much higher level within the organizational structure and also encourages the kinds of administrative support that will be needed to carry out an effective public relations effort. Further, it suggests that educational preparation would appropriately be found in management-type courses as well as courses of a more specific nature.

Public relations can also be viewed as the effort to enhance the image of the organization in the eyes of consumers or other publics. A library needs to position its overall image in the local community and regional market in much the same way as does any other business. In reality, 'public relations' is an accurate descriptor — the relations an organization has with its various publics or target markets.

In a very real sense, public relations is both more and less than the promotion component of a full marketing plan. It can be seen as the communication module which serves the promotion function; conversely, it may just as easily be depicted as a philosophical relationship between library and community which serves as a guiding light for promotional activities. For the purposes of this chapter, the following hierarchical progression will be used (see Figure 1):

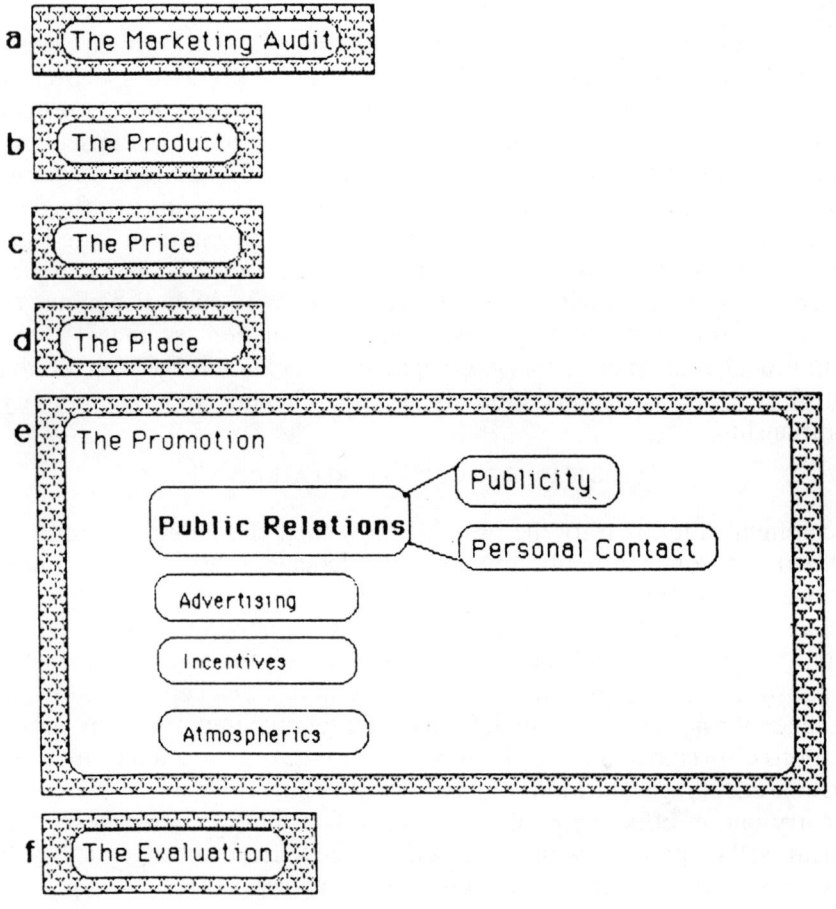

FIGURE 1: *The role of public relations in the marketing process.* (Note: Elements of the planning process are not pictured).

1. The process of marketing includes six major components:
   a. *The marketing audit* — a snapshot in time of external and internal environments with an eye to identifying strengths, limitations, threats and opportunities; an assessment of needs in both the library and the community served.
   b. *The product* — materials, access channels and programmes, the range of which is directly related to organizational mission and goals.
   c. *The price* — the cost required to produce a product, including both direct and indirect costs.
   d. *The place* — how the product will be distributed; the channel that links product and consumer.
   e. *The promotion* — communication of information and benefits to target groups.
   f. *The evaluation* — the monitoring of how the marketing/planning process is progressing and a final assessment of how well everything worked.
2. Public relations will be situated as a subset of promotion (e), along with *advertising* (paid publicity), *incentives* (opportunities such as free online search, designed to encourage client use), and *atmospherics* (the ambience and environment of distribution channels).
3. For further clarification, public relations itself can be subdivided into *publicity* (low or no cost news coverage, such as that generated through press releases, newsletters, bookmarks, posters and displays) and *personal contact* (that one-to-one contact between library staff and clients).

The traditional view of libraries on marketing (and public relations as a component of marketing) has been in terms of promotion only — and promotion in the sense that the libraries' products are so intrinsically valuable that people 'should' use them and therefore only need to be alerted to their existence. In addition, since promotion has tended to focus on programmatic activities, such as film showings and story hours, rather than on the full range of services, it has not succeeded in informing the community even at this partial level. Most clients have a very poor sense of what they have a right to expect — and demand — from libraries.[3]

This traditional view is grounded in large part in the attitudes held and projected by librarians themselves. This limited scope and perspective has cheated both libraries and communities over time, as libraries are tremendous community resources which have been dramatically under-used and consequently under-valued. Operating in the realm of 'intrinsic value' as opposed to the identification and satisfying of client needs, libraries have struggled valiantly to survive in years of economic hardship and, today, are beginning to lose the struggle. The economic health of libraries, if not survival itself, may well depend upon the use of marketing and planning strategies, communicated through effective public relations, to significantly alter the perceived role and position of the library in society.

Therefore, since these perceptions are found in staff attitudes, the logical and most reasonable place to begin encouraging attitudinal change is in the library school as students are initially learning about library services (and, of course, in continuing education programmes for existing staff). In fairness, the curriculum revision efforts of many library schools have attempted minor surgery on the problem. In reality, however, major changes are required in an attempt to move radically from the notion of intrinsic value to the satisfying of client needs. Public relations may well be the most important of the concepts to be learned because its roots are in the attitudes of library staff members, and the other promotional elements will flow quite readily from a proactive attitude.

What kinds of changes could reasonably be effected in the library school curriculum? In practical terms, much is dependent on faculty perceptions of library service. In an ideal world, each course syllabus could be designed with an active component relating to attitude. Upon entering library school, each student would be required to take an entry course in which the role of libraries in the information age and the opportunities made available by developing technologies would be emphasized. Stress would be placed on client needs, the importance of serving as a link in a worldwide information network, the impossibility of being all things to all people and the corresponding mandate to identify target markets. Specific skills, such as bibliographic organization, reference, collection development and management strategies, would still be integral to the curriculum, but they would be taught in the context of the library's mission in the community — as opposed to being regarded as internal skills. In other words, the entire curricular focus would be looking outward from the library to its community (and specific target markets), rather than focusing inward on task-specific operations.

Outrageous? Unworkable? Too idealistic? Not at all. Just as a glass can be perceived as either half full or half empty, the perceptions which library schools instil in students will influence their approach to library service for years to come. It is certainly possible to re-learn, but it is much easier to learn a proactive attitude initially than to try to unlearn old ways before new ones can be adequately assimilated. It is not unreasonable to assume that many schools regarded their academic role as a concentration on knowledge and skills. It is equally reasonable to postulate that schools seeking to educate librarians qualified and capable of coping with a rapidly changing society and an explosion in both volume of information and technological applications will need increasingly to focus attention on attitude development in order to facilitate coping strategies.

DESIGNING THE PUBLIC INFORMATION PLAN

The library's mission is the philosophical base which supports the entire public relations effort. Written in sand and not stone, the mission is a simple statement of purpose and intent that is designed to communicate what the library does and why to both the internal staff and the external community. The rationale for this statement must be frequently defended (at least annually during budget hearings) — and be capable of being defended! The mission is the first swamp that many library managers stumble into, and is more often than not comprised of simple platitudes that say little and mean less. All too often, library staffs are not clear as to the library's role *vis-a-vis* the community; clients and potential clients are almost never sure. It is not at all absurd to state that most members of any given community will not have even a partial idea of the full range of services that they have a right to expect and demand from their library (whether that library be public, academic, special or school). The down side of this reality is that the library may then not be regarded as an essential service — why should it? — and consequently will not receive adequate funding when economic conditions become tight.

Conversely, the library that is proactive, seeking out and responding to client needs in an accurate and timely fashion, is also a library that probably communicates in a two-way mode with its target markets — i.e., doing a good job of establishing high quality public relations.

How should this communication take place? There are several communication questions:

1. What is to be communicated? And why?

As discussed above, the library's mission and role(s) in the community need to be primary topics of communication. The Public Library Association (a division of the American Library Association), in its Public Library Development Project, has created two manuals of options and procedures entitled, *Planning and role setting for public libraries* and *Output measures for public libraries,* 2nd ed.[4] Although designed for public libraries, the concepts presented in these manuals can be generalised to other types of libraries. The manuals serve as guides in determining how the library will relate to its community and, at the other end of the funnel, examine the outputs that were achieved as a measure of that relationship.

Beyond the dialogue regarding mission and role(s), the correlation to formulated goals, objectives and priorities needs to be continually communicated. Not only 'why' the library exists needs to be articulated, but also the strategies that are in place to help it fulfil its *raison d'etre*. It is rather similar to the relationship between old friends — that friendship would not survive if it were not nurtured with regularity so that all parties participated in a common and shared understanding.

2. To whom?

All members of the library's community have a right to be kept informed and knowledgeable, but it is the identified target markets who deserve the most specialized communication. Since attempting to serve the nebulous 'everyone' is no longer workable management practice, the full range of potential target markets needs to be ascertained and a selection of those markets designated for particular concentrated effort during each planning period. These designated target markets may vary from year to year; some may remain fairly stable. However, the choice of target markets must be tied to information gleaned from the marketing audit and, since environmental conditions vary, designated markets will logically vary as well.

3. How?

Communication can be designed to use a variety of communication channels. The mass media (a probable stable target market in itself) should be cultivated so that messages are distributed with regularity; publicity mechanisms such as news releases, special events, and brochures can be employed. All aspects of promotion described earlier in the chapter can be utilised as appropriate. The specific choices are simply tools; the motivation to communicate is the prime mover.

4. Who has the responsibility?

This can be a sticky question. Various administrative approaches have attempted to use: a committee structure, assignment to a key management person, designation of a staff member, or an assumption that 'everyone should do it'. There are elements of truth in all of these strategies, but there are two key axioms that will make or break the effort:

    a. One person should have the overall responsibility; and

    b. All staff members need to feel — and perform — as if they were part of an active task force of good will ambassadors (who smile a lot!)

The educational implications of the above discussions are many. The earlier comments regarding the injection of attitude formation and proactive motivation into the library school curriculum are still eminently applicable. Beyond this approach, however, are additional curricular concerns that deserve attention.

In order to communicate effectively, with both clarity and style, many, if not most, students would benefit from instruction in communication skills, both written and oral. The use of language to forge common and informed understanding is a difficult and sometimes ambiguous activity. Novices without adequate training in language use may do more harm than good, since mis-information or only one-way communication can create unfortunate barriers. The ability to manipulate language is a true talent in a prospective library staff member, particularly when specific target markets are to receive unique messages.

As a complement to language skills, the ability to create audiovisual representations of the message or graphic highlights as emphasis can be of great benefit to a library. Students who have the opportunity to learn media production techniques will be able to use those skills in a whole spectrum of ways, from simple posters or bulletin boards to dynamic and interesting annual and budget reports. Most library schools, if they offer opportunities in this area at all, relegate this type of course to elective status. The importance of being able to communicate in tune with the receiver's preferred learning style is only starting to be recognised, often as a result of research into learning disabilities. The librarian of the future would be better served if the capability to communicate in all media were part of his or her essential repertoire of knowledge and skills.

In addition to these various approaches to teaching communication skills, the importance of research skills must also be recognised. All marketing and planning efforts are predicated on data which is secured through a marketing audit — which is a research process. Good managerial decision-making should also be grounded in hard data as well as intuition. When research skills are not part of the formal and, hopefully, required library school curriculum, graduates enter the profession with a significant limitation. It might be proposed that continuing education could fill this gap, and well it might — if librarians were disposed to do so. However, all too frequently, librarians are humanities graduates and seem to avoid any courses that suggest learning mathematics, statistics, or anything quantitative. It therefore seems incumbent upon library schools to assure that research capability will be part of the knowledge package of every graduate by designing research concepts and skills as required coursework.

Finally, both communication and research skills serve well the marketing/planning process — of which public relations is an important component. Specific knowledge and skills are also needed in marketing/planning. The management expertise that is able to organise and facilitate such a process is best acquired not simply through experience but also through the theoretical and philosophical lessons of initial professional education. More and more library schools are including management courses as part of the required curriculum; planning is becoming a more frequently found element in these courses. However, marketing is still a dark horse and receives little attention — which means that public relations is unlikely to be taught in the context of the total marketing process. This unfortunate situation tends to result in a view of public relations as more closely related to simple publicity, ignoring its very real complexities and ramifications.

It is interesting to note that if a library school were to seriously include marketing/planning as an essential management tool in its required curriculum, one of the probable side effects would be the shift of attitude from the notion of intrinsic value to that of consumer need discussed earlier in this Chapter. The inclusion of courses dealing with communication and research skills would strengthen this attitudinal shift. The correlation among these various curricular elements is a marked one.

ADMINISTRATIVE SUPPORTS FOR PUBLIC RELATIONS

In order to mount and continue an effective marketing effort, there must be an understanding at the top management level that this is a long-term, ongoing activity. A philosophical commitment should be put in writing in terms of a formal resolution; however, financial support also needs to be demonstrated in order to fully activate the project. The formal resolution should include language regarding the following categories: (i) The need for staff training; (ii) Co-operation with other groups; (iii) Information appearances around the community; (iv) Promotional literature; (v) Designation of a staff co-ordinator; (vi) Educational implications. The mandage for both pre-service and continuing education is specified in items 1 and 6, and implied in the rest of the list. Items (ii) and (iii) reflect attitudinal concerns, since traditional views place the librarian within the library in a caretaker capacity at all times. Number (iv) addresses the need for communication skills and (v) illustrates both managerial attitude and a knowledge of managerial processes.

The need for education is inexorably linked to the ability to function effectively in the world of work. Administration has the responsibility to provide both philosophical and financial support; however, the professional commitment to excellence would also demand that administrative expectations and needs be communicated to library schools so that both educators and practitioners are working together towards a common goal: educating graduates who are competent to contribute needed knowledge, skills and attitudes to the profession-at-large and employing libraries in particular.

CONCLUSION

If public relations is to be implemented for maximum effect, its placement must be within a total marketing/planning process that is understood and supported by administration, professional staff and support staff. This happy situation is best and most easily achieved if the personnel involved have been educated at the pre-service level in the concepts of proactive attitude, communication, research and marketing/planning which have been the focus of this Chapter. This goal, however worthy, is still an ideal and, in today's world, must be supplemented by continuing education of existing staff who did not receive this education at the level of initial preparation. Future curriculum design should reflect the importance of these concepts in order to prepare professionals who can not only cope with change, but use it to best advantage. It is an exciting and challenging time to be an information professional.

REFERENCES

1. NITECKI, D.A. Competencies required of public services librarians to use new technologies. In: Linda C. Smith, ed. *Professional competencies — technology and the librarian*. Urbana-Champaign: University of Illinois Graduate School of Library and Information Science, 1983, 44.
2. KIES, C. *Marketing and public relations for libraries*. Metuchen, NJ and London: Scarecrow Press, Inc., 4-5.
3. WEINGAND, D.E. *Marketing/planning library and information services*. Littleton, CO: Libraries Unlimited, 1987, 110.
4. *Planning and role setting for public libraries*. Chicago and London: American Library Association, 1987.
   Output measures for public libraries, 2nd ed. Chicago and London: American Library Association, 1987.

CHAPTER EIGHT
TRAINING AND EDUCATING STAFF FOR PUBLIC RELATIONS
Jon Pyle

No library service of any size can reliably deliver an effective service to its clients unless someone is specifically and practically responsible for its public relations and promotional activities. Every single member of staff has an important role to play in library PR practice. Consequently PR training and education are permanently vital, from the top to the bottom of your organisation.

This chapter aims to support these assertions on the basis of practical experience. So two disclaimers are called for. First, I do not mean to imply that Sheffield City Libraries, my employers, are world leaders in library PR and promotion. Some things we do well, others we know we could do better — and we're trying to improve. Secondly, although examples that follow are drawn from my own public library experience, I am not forgetting other types of library. Even when the clientele and organisational background are different, the principles and practice remain basically the same.

ON HAVING A POLICY

Successful PR and promotional practice depends on continuous attention to the library's relationships with its various publics. That sort of continuity is only possible with the help of staff who can devote their full-time attention to the matter. In Sheffield we were fortunate, initially by historical accident but subsequently by design, to find ourselves with someone in that position. A restructuring exercise later gave us the chance to formalise the situation, draw up a new job description and appoint a professional graphic designer to our publicity unit.

At about the same time, a new statement of the library service's objectives strongly emphasised responsiveness to changing community needs and expectations — so the service was now firmly and officially market oriented. But of course this is nothing new. What counts is how well the reality will measure up to the good intentions — which are all too easily subverted by a performance that continues to go perversely in all the wrong directions. Sheffield's management team tried to counter this danger by introducing educational seminars and discussion sessions with staff at various levels in the organisation. They dealt with aspects of policy, including priorities for an effective service, racism awareness, materials selection criteria and performance measurement.

A *Staff guidance manual* was devised, which, among other things, set out policies and procedures on subjects ranging from procedures during severe weather conditions to guidelines on hospitality from commercial organisations. For the first time all staff had easy access to policy information and advice, plus contact points for further information if they needed it.

But what had all that got to do with PR training? — it made it much easier. Three policy instructions on publicity and promotion procedures, media relations and policy statements to the media could now act as reference points for our attempts to educate staff to follow policy. But we don't say, 'You must do this because it's policy'; we say, 'It's to your advantage to do this because it will make your job easier in these ways . . .'

Our policy in practice

1. All publicity materials are written, designed, produced and issued by the Library's publicity unit. Even unavoidable, instant emergency notices are written on purpose-designed emergency notice blanks.
2. Major promotional events are co-ordinated wholly or partly by the publicity unit.
3. All press releases are written, produced, targeted and distributed by the unit.
4. Exhibits for local shows, carnivals and festivals are co-ordinated by a staff working group convened by the unit.
5. All forthcoming events organised in, by or for any of our libraries are notified to the unit on purpose-designed cards — from which they are transferred to a word processor file as a source for published lists and programmes.
6. The publicity unit helps service points with major promotional display or exhibition projects.
7. If approached by the media, staff are encouraged to give factual information and to be as helpful as possible — but to refer questions on matters of policy to the appropriate members of the management team.

Our publicity unit treats other staff as clients. We talk to them about their publicity requirements, and if necessary explain to them why what they thought they wanted is not what they need. The learning process is two-way. We visit groups of staff from time to time both to explain how we can help them promote their services and to find out how they would like us to improve the way we work for them. Our role is supportive of the library service's objectives, and we think we have a big advantage in being part of the library organisation. We know quite a lot about how libraries work, and our librarian colleagues know they can talk with us whenever they want to.

Where a public library has to work with a Council PR office there often seems to be a comprehension gap; the librarians know nothing about PR and the PR people know nothing about libraries. The results can be disastrous. For example, the library can produce an awful text for a publicity leaflet and, due to lack of communication with its originators and possibly a bit of intellectual laziness brought on by pressure of work, the PR office can dress it up with attractive graphics, print it nicely and end up with a leaflet that looks pretty but actually puts people off using the library.

Because our unit is part of Sheffield's libraries department we don't have that sort of problem. We can phone up the author and say, "We can see what you're trying to do, but it won't work this way because . . . So how about trying this way instead?" Our clients don't mind — they appreciate that publicity is our job, and they learn fast. Because we are accessible, because we keep them aware of what we can do, because they keep seeing all the publicity material and news releases we produce, Sheffield's staff are far more publicity-minded than they were five or six years ago. It's now second nature to tell the publicity unit about a planned event, and to start thinking about publicity and promotion for a new service as soon as the service is first mooted.[1]

It wasn't always so. For example, when a new branch library opened (several years ago) no-one thought to order any printed publicity at all until ten days beforehand. A badly written, tedious brochure for the attending dignitaries was rushed to the printers, who threw it together (untouched by any designer) and delivered the appalling result with half a day to spare. No-one knew any better. When our next new library opens, the publicity print will have been thought about for over a year, and written and produced by professionals well in advance of opening day. So in Sheffield we are doing all we can to raise staff awareness of publicity and promotion, using our publicity unit's resources and the policies that back them up.

But do your staff need to know about the theory of marketing and PR (which, of course, takes in far more than publicity)? In my view, not unless they want to. As long as the management has access to marketing and PR expertise, it can justify all the right moves by explaining objectives and the way these actions will help to achieve them. The jargon can be more a barrier than an aid to persuasion. As long as the staff know, or can easily find out, where they stand on matters of library policy, the very existence of an internal publicity or PR office or person makes effective local PR much easier for them. They know which publics they most need to reach with their services — or at least they do when prompted to do some hard thinking — and clear lines of responsibility mean that they can bring forward ideas for events or print or advertising and be sure of advice and support. They don't have to go out on a limb, doing their own publicity with little skill and no assurance of approval. So they can keep coming up with ideas and keep learning, by experience and some simple research, which promotional techniques work best in their own geographical or subject areas.

ESSENTIAL SKILLS FOR LIBRARY PROMOTION

Let us assume that your library manager has read this far, made you responsible for publicity and promotion, and given you time and resources to carry out that promotion. If you are in a one or two person special library, let's assume that you have told yourself that promotion is vital (see Matarazzo's *Closing the corporate library*[2] if you need proof) and have decided to stop doing some other chore to leave yourself time — in other words, the organisation and the will are there.

Now you need to learn a lot, and fast. In publicity and PR you never stop learning, but a librarian thrown in at the deep end has to realise that he or she knows virtually nothing about the job. When I look back at some of the press releases and amateur graphics I was responsible for five or six years ago — well, I'm embarrassed. Unfortunately, too many libraries are still at the pre-embarrassed stage.

At the end of this chapter is a very select list of essential books. Librarians, of all people, have every opportunity to read about the publicity skills they need; public relations, marketing, graphic design, advertising, copywriting, media relations. You soon learn to distinguish among books on library publicity and to tell whether they were written by someone who really knew the subject or by a well-intentioned but profoundly ill-equipped librarian. The latter are in the majority, I'm sorry to say. There is so much to learn that it's unreasonable to expect every head of department or branch librarian to know it; which is why, however much you may try to educate your staff, uncontrolled, unco-ordinated publicity is bound to be patchy, wasteful and shamefully unprofessional.

So you are in charge. What are the skills you can learn? Probably marketing — or a grasp of the basic principles that can be found in a thousand textbooks[3] — and public relations practice,[4] which is an integral part of good management. There is no room and no reason to go further into either here; read the books, go on the courses. Which are the skills you will almost certainly need to buy rather than try to practise yourself? Just cast an eye over a random sample of library publicity print and there are two inescapable answers. Graphic design and copywriting.

Graphic design

Libraries and information services have to compete in their chosen markets, often against commercial opposition that finds it profitable to commission advertising and publicity of a very high standard from professional agencies, writers and designers. If those libraries try to compete using leaflets written by an assistant librarian and designed by the person on the staff who was quite good at drawing at school, what chance do they have of success?

Graphic design is a term encompassing a number of skills — which do not necessarily include being particularly good at freehand drawing. They do include a knowledge of the principles of layout, typography, reprographics, printing techniques and their applications, paper technology, colour theory, graphics equipment and technology, illustrative sources and techniques, packaging design, and much more. Graphic design is a skilled job for a trained specialist, and there is no getting round that fact. "But we can't afford to pay a designer. What can I do?" The first move, sometimes inexplicably overlooked, is to seek out expertise within your own parent organisation. Many local councils have a PR or publicity department with its own design office that could do work for libraries. Colleges, polytechnics and universities often have design, print or reprographic services (or teaching departments) that could help. Semi-external services like these are likely to be slower; but important publicity can be planned well in advance if you train the right people to think ahead and work to long deadlines.

The second move is to train your staff to use their eyes — to analyse how graphic design is used all around them, every day. If the people responsible for ninety per cent of current library publicity print had only done that, their efforts would not have escaped into the outside world to destroy the credibility of the services they are supposed to be promoting. A critical awareness of advertising, TV, magazine, poster and leaflet graphics will reveal the skill that goes into effective design and the way that even the simplest ideas are meticulously worked out and executed.

In the same way, an observant stroll round a John Lewis, Habitat, Sainsbury or Asda store demonstrates how important co-ordinated graphic design is in guiding customers to their destinations; that is, delivering a service.[5] How many libraries match that standard? To get a little closer to it, you could start by organising your own training, assisted by a professional designer. First, your staff will realise how little they know about design, which is a good start. Secondly, they can learn to recognise the factors like ideas, shape, layout, proportion and colour that contribute to successful design. Instant graphic designers will not emerge; but at least you may find your staff looking to skilled help before rushing posters and leaflets into print, and producing simple, acceptable displays without the 'aid' of magic markers and hand lettering. From time to time courses for librarians, with titles like 'Publicity on a shoestring', try to communicate a basic grasp of simple graphic techniques, equipment, dry transfer lettering and so forth. As long as there are libraries that persist in the self-destructive belief that promotion is a frippery, such courses will continue to be a regrettable necessity if anything at all is to be done to raise standards. But they should be the last resort of the desperate, after every attempt to acquire proper graphics expertise has failed; not an easy but an inadequate option.

So far we have been talking about the appearance of print and display; but what about the words?

EDUCATION AND TRAINING OF STAFF

Copywriting

Publicity copywriting is another specialised skill, which demands a particular kind of flair for language — and plenty of practice. A good introduction to the qualities that make a successful copywriter is Alastair Crompton's *Do your own advertising*.[6] If you are the person in charge of publicity, you will need to find someone who has these skills to write, or at least vet, all your library's adverts, posters, leaflets, flyers, bookmarks, reminder letters, moving message displays and news releases (which are an art in themselves). Everything that the library produces in any form of print affects its image in the recipient's mind, and it all deserves careful attention.

As I have already implied, the copywriter and the designer need to work together if the result is not to resemble an unsuccessful game of consequences. A PPRG day school, first run in July 1987, illustrated that point. Called 'Making leaflets work', it passed publicity leaflets supplied by the participating libraries to a team of copywriters and designers, who reworked them and presented the results to the course delegates, inviting comments and criticism. Demand for places on the day school far exceeded capacity, and the delegates who were there responded so positively and enthusiastically that the contents were expanded into a very popular book.[7]

This and other PPRG events have proved that there is an encouraging demand among UK librarians for high quality education in PR-related subjects. One of the attractions is the fact that good PR can be practised at any level in every aspect of library work. One of the lessons of the leaflets course, that marketing theories can and should be applied to originating an item as small and apparently simple as a leaflet for new library members, underlines the vital role of the library's publicity person. It should be his or her role to know that principle, and to educate other staff to understand it.

But before we start writing and designing publicity for our services, don't we have to identify and understand our target publics? Naturally we do.

LEARNING ABOUT RESEARCH

What library managers want from research is practical, useful information about topics like market trends, the social profile of local communities, and public awareness and perceptions of library services. They need that research to be rigorously planned and executed using sound sampling methods. They need it to deliver reliable conclusions that can help them answer questions like "What business am I in?", "How will I know when I achieve my objectives?", "What should be my next objectives?". They know it has to be reasonably well funded to have a fair chance of fulfilling those needs.

What they are more likely to get from research is 'free' amateur local surveys by their own staff, probably with ill-focused questions and unreliable results. Libraries generally don't have the money to commission professional market research on local services. The only help they are likely to get from the market research organisations is the marginally useful information from the polls of public attitudes to and use of local services that are occasionally commissioned by individual local authorities.

Sheffield City Libraries Research Assistant Alan Beevers aims to make the local DIY research more useful to managers. One of his roles is to enable and encourage middle managers to take on their own research, with sound methodology and properly thought through objectives.[8] A typical example was a recent project in the Arts and Social Science library in Sheffield Central Library, designed simply to discover what current users were using the service for and what groups they might fall into for the purposes of reviewing future services for them. Alan Beevers sees this kind of small-scale research being as much a training exercise as an immediate management aid. Much of its value lies in the way it encourages staff to think analytically about the performance and purpose of their service — to remember about marketing and public relations as well as the mechanics of running a library. But it can also deliver an important lesson in the perverse ways of messy, illogical reality. Where the research conclusions ought to lead to changes in the service, an apparently irrational high-level decision or the opposition of a councillor or governor can get those conclusions ignored. The researcher can easily turn cynical in the circumstances, and no wonder; but there is a positive lesson to be learned. Planning and carrying out research in itself requires PR expertise. Decision makers should be kept aware of the project's progress and made to feel involved. Researchers should present their recommendations in a way that relates them to the organisation's stated objectives; so that saying 'no' demands a good explanation.

TRAINING FOR THE FUTURE

So far we have been looking mostly at pragmatic forms of training and education for staff. Problem — library displays are feeble; response — display courses for staff concerned. Problem — staff are unaware of the publicity help available to them; response — publicity presentations at staff group meetings.

The advantage of pragmatic training is that it is quite evidently relevant to immediate need. The disadvantage is that before the need becomes obvious the library has to have been doing something badly, and someone on the staff has to realise this, decide to take action, and contrive to get the training organised. The process may take a long time — and often does. We could all quote examples from our own experience here — but I will claim my right to silence and leave you to recall the skeletons from your own cupboards.

EDUCATION AND TRAINING OF STAFF

Even so, the more adaptable and responsive your service, the more reactive training you will be organising. As I have already tried to illustrate, the library's own staff is one of its most important publics. PR practice is about establishing understanding between the organisation and its publics, so good internal communication on policies and procedures is vital: communication, not instruction, because staff have to understand and support the reasons for procedures. Otherwise, at the contact point with the service user, the counter or phone, a 'don't blame me — I can't understand it either'' attitude is liable to develop. Once disillusionment sets in it is infectious, and the result is bad customer relations. A mundane but, I suspect, very common instance is the book reservation service. How many public and academic libraries advertise a service that they cannot efficiently deliver, with the result that harassed counter staff and annoyed customers jointly and severally rubbish it?

But if reactive, pragmatic training is not enough on its own, how can we train to make the library's PR performance as good as possible to start with? I suggest we have to take a medium term view and train for the library services of the future. If standards of awareness of and practice in library PR, marketing, design and promotion can be raised, the prospects for an effective, responsive, necessary library network for the 1990s and beyond are bound to improve.

The main objective of the Library Association's Publicity and Public Relations Group is to raise just those standards. It aims to achieve it by acting as an information forum for its members, and by organising day and weekend schools for the library and information profession that make a point of bringing in experts from outside the library world to put library PR into context. The President of the Institute of Public Relations, a Design Co-ordinator from the John Lewis Partnership, the ex-Director of Public Relations from the Greater London Council, experts in information technology, graphic design, printing and marketing, a national magazine editor, the Marketing Director of Madam Tussauds . . . and others.

Libraries, themselves information centres, can be surprisingly slow to apply outside information to reshaping their own management processes. That has to change, or they lose touch with accelerating social and technological development. But if some senior library managers are at this very moment too busy polishing the obsolete machinery below decks to notice that the tide has gone out and beached them, maybe some PR and marketing knowledge will equip their successors for a salvage operation. If the success of the PPRG so far is anything to go by, there is good reason for hope.

AND THE MORAL OF THAT IS...

The mutual understanding between the library and its publics that PR aims to achieve is bound to result in services that reach more people and give them more of what they need, the aims of good management. Planned PR practice is part of good management; so are good external and internal communications, and customer relations training for the staff delivering the services.

To learn to excel in all these departments, your library could, if it were very rich, hardly do better than to invest in a complete set of Video Arts training videos. The Video Arts company is itself an excellent example of the results of expert marketing and promotion. Because a group of people with TV writing, production and performance skills identified a specialised market for their services, developed a new medium for staff training to new levels of competence and creativity, and promoted the results to the right people, Video Arts is virtually synonymous with video-led training. Customers will pay the high purchase and hire charges because the product is what they need and they are confident of its quality.

Your library service, you may say, is a much better bargain. Maybe so, but are your clients so confident of the quality of the product? Are you homing in so accurately on the needs of your publics? Are you using specialist communications skills to reach them? almost certainly, the honest answers are don't know, no, and not enough. I refer you back to the first two sentences of this chapter, and rest my case.

REFERENCES

1. SHEFFIELD CITY LIBRARIES. *The library book*. Sheffield: Sheffield City Libraries, 1987.
   A cartoon guide for libraries on how, and why, to organise successful community arts events in libraries — including publicity planning and selecting target audiences.
2. MATARAZZO, J.M. *Closing the corporate library: case-studies on the decision-making process*. Washington: Special Libraries Association, 1981. *A revealing examination of the reasons for in-house library closures. Poor communications and lack of promotion feature strongly.*
3. DAVIDSON, J.H. *Offensive marketing* 2nd ed. Harmondsworth: Penguin, 1987.
4. HAYWOOD, R. *All about PR*. London: McGraw, 1984.
   Probably the best PR handbook available. The author's infectious enthusiasm shines through, and the information content is very well organised, with useful checklists at the end of chapters.
5. OLINS, W. *The corporate personality*. London: Design Council, 1978.
   A fascinating exploration of visual corporate identity as the expression of an organisation's 'personality', by the founder of one of the world's leading design consultancies.
6. CROMPTON, A. *Do your own advertising*. Gold Farthing Press, 1985.
   Intended for the small business person, but equally applicable to libraries, a down-to-earth guide to the basics of good copywriting and the elements that make up advertising and publicity print. Very readable. The same author's The craft of copywriting *is more for the ad-industry professional but almost equally useful.*
7. PYLE, J. and HARRINGTON, S. *Making leaflets work*. London: Library Association Publicity and PR Group, 1988.

EDUCATION AND TRAINING OF STAFF

8. MOORE, N. *How to do research.* 2nd ed. London: Library Association Publishing Ltd. 1987. *A basic guide for the total newcomer to library research.*

Recommended periodicals

Campaign, the advertising weekly. A valuable source of ideas, and an eye-opening record of the feverish effort that goes into every stage of an advertising campaign.

Public Relations is the official journal of the Institute of Public Relations, valuable for its case-histories and articles on PR tools such as the communications audit, political lobbying and media relations.

*Public Ey*e is the newsletter of the Publicity and Public Relations Group of the Library Association (PPRG).

CHAPTER NINE
EVALUATING A CAMPAIGN PROGRAMME
WILL IT WORK, IS IT WORKING, HAS IT WORKED... WHY?
David Pickton

THE NEED FOR EVALUATION
"I know you believe you understand what you think I said, but I am not sure you realise that what you heard is not what I meant."

Simplistically, the need for campaign evaluation is self-evident, we want to know whether our promotions have worked. In the world of communications, the chances of being misunderstood or misinterpreted are probably greater than those of 'getting it right'. We not only want to know whether our communications (promotions) have been received, but to what extent they have been understood as we intended them to be, and if not, why not. The justification for evaluation resides in the knowledge of money well spent or, in the case of failure, what not to do in the future.

The process of evaluation, therefore, becomes much more complex than merely reviewing the outcome of a campaign at its completion and should at least address the questions:

Can we expect our campaign to be successful?

Is our campaign currently working?

Has our campaign been successful — why and to what extent?

Implied in these questions is an extremely important point which is worth stating explicitly. Campaign evaluation may be undertaken prior to campaign launch and during the campaign period as well as at its completion, a view shared by Douglas Wood, Marketing Manager, Aslib.[1] This permits the modification of material and campaign design both before and, if necessary, during the programme with corresponding savings in resources as well as an increased chance of success.

All organisations have limited resources and it therefore becomes imperative that those resources are used wisely and with greatest effect. The development and implementation of promotional campaigns is not a science. Indeed, often it is not even scientific in nature. However, this is not an argument against carrying out evaluation but rather, an argument which highlights the need for evaluation if any attempt at all is to be made to be economical, efficient and effective in campaign promotions. There are costs to be incurred in undertaking evaluation exercises and there can be no guarantee of success for any campaign. No amount of evaluation can create such certainty. What it can do, however, is to increase the chance of success and reduce the potential waste of resources spent on campaign failure.

Some years ago, Blaise Cronin, then a member of the Aslib Research and Consultancy Division, presented a paper at the Aslib Conference, 'Promoting and publicising library and information services'.[2] In his presentation he made a plea for greater campaign evaluation, a plea which was supported by what he called 'the cumulative advantage theory of promotion'. Allan Whatley expressed this same theory in the following way:

> 'If one accepts the theory that nothing succeeds like success then the more business a library can attract the more likely it is to win the attention of the public and more support from the local council: the more issues, the more inquiries, the more public demand and thereby irrefutable evidence that the service justifies greater resources'.[3]

Of course, this argument applies equally well to all library services, not just public libraries and, if promotional campaigns are made more effective through systematic evaluation, then the more likely the theory is to apply. As Cronin put it,

> 'Effective promotion has a snowballing effect and, in a sense, feeds off its own achievements'.[4]

Further weight is given to this argument by Patricia Berger's research,[5] in which she found a positive correlation between the level and sophistication of public relations activities and library budget allocations.

The process of evaluation, then, has a double advantage. First, it provides the means by which promotional campaigns may be made more effective. Secondly, it delivers the measures which may be used to support the case for increased library provision.

How much evaluation?

The size and nature of campaign programmes can vary enormously and, as such, consideration does need to be given to the amount of resources allocated to the evaluation programmes which should accompany them.

For campaigns involving minimal costs (whether these be in terms of finance, facilities, staff or time) there may be some merit in the argument that investing disproportionate resources in evaluation is not cost effective. It should also be recognised, though, that evaluation is a constructive exercise whereby knowledge and experience is built up over time. The results of evaluating one campaign should reveal lessons to be learned for future activities, provided it is realised that such lessons cannot be simplistically applied to novel situations without some re-interpretation and re-application. An evaluation programme may justifiably be considered an investment for now and the future, the building of knowledge and experience which may be put to good use in the design of forthcoming campaigns.

For libraries it is important to temper the possible with the practical and in this context accuracy, validity and reliability need to be considered. In simple terms this may be stated as the degree of faith and trust which may be placed in the information derived from campaign evaluation and the need for a balance to be sought between the effort expended and the quality of results obtained.

Can a campaign ever be fully evaluated? The answer is probably no.

> 'Evaluation will never provide all the answers. What it can do — and this is no minor contribution — is to expose the failings of existing programs and point out the need for change.'[6]

There will always be questions unasked and unanswered. There will always be limitations of finance, time, staff, facilities and expertise as well as the limitations of the techniques available. A campaign is invariably subject to a myriad uncontrolled variables, including all those environmental factors prevailing at the time of the campaign, as well as those which have gone before. But this is not to decry evaluation. There may be few unequivocally right answers, but this should not dissuade the campaigner from the search. Campaign evaluation has value, if not in guaranteeing success, at least in reducing the risk of failure in both current and future campaigns. If undertaken wisely, evaluation can lead to economy, efficiency and effectiveness of effort.

In 1979 Paul Sykes wrote, 'At no time has the importance of intelligent promotion of public libraries been greater than at present'.[7] That time has not passed, it is still as true today and applies to all library services. Whether it is used as a means of obtaining greater resources directly or indirectly through Cronin's cumulative advantage theory, or as a means of maintaining the *status quo* in situations which would otherwise lead to a contraction of services, the operative words 'intelligent promotion' of libraries hinge on the need for feedback and evaluation.

What can be evaluated?

Before considering techniques of evaluation it is important and necessary to explore the nature of what it is we are really examining when evaluating a promotional campaign, that is to say, the communications process and the consequential effects it may have on our actions. By briefly reviewing this process, a greater appreciation and understanding may be achieved not only of campaign design but also of the variety of approaches and techniques used in campaign evaluation and the reasons for their adoption. The following sections attempt to foster this understanding.

WHAT IS A CAMPAIGN PROGRAMME?

A promotional campaign may be described as 'a series of planned and co-ordinated promotional activities directed at specific targets and designed to achieve one or more goals, aims or objectives'. By implication the activities should be complementary and synergistic such that when implemented they successively move towards the ultimate fulfilment of the objectives selected.

A series of promotional activities — The promotional mix

For a campaign to warrant the term 'campaign' an appropriate range of promotional activities and a balance between them should be sought. The term, 'promotional mix' is often used to describe this range of promotions. A single promotional act does not of itself justify the title, 'campaign', and worse still may heighten the chance of failure through over-reliance on its single activity. The success or otherwise of a campaign is at least partly dependent on the choice of promotional mix and the synergy achieved between its component parts. In evaluating a campaign, consideration should be given to the mix and the quality of promotional activities used.

Planning

All activities need to be planned in advance of implementation while still maintaining flexibility. Some libraries plan the major and most costly activities in fine detail whilst allowing room for manoeuvre in smaller promotions and the ability to respond to unforeseen opportunities and threats. Without careful planning a campaign may go sadly astray by not fulfilling its purpose and, perhaps in the process, going over budget.

Co-ordination

Co-ordination of promotional activities should be a natural consequence of careful planning. It is clearly necessary, as a campaign uses a range of promotions and utilises a range of resources including people, facilities and materials. Without co-ordination there is a danger of losing the synergistic effect of the promotional mix and the campaign failing through poor implementation. The evaluation process should consider not only the design of a campaign in terms of the range of promotions planned but also the degree to which those plans come to fruition.

Identification of specific targets

A campaign may ultimately fail not so much through poor planning or implementation but through inaccurate focusing upon a campaign audience. It is necessary to specify clearly the target group or groups of people the campaign is intended to reach and influence. Without such targeting there is every likelihood that both the content and the media chosen for the campaign will not be appropriate. Moreover, limited and precious resources may be wasted as a consequence. In evaluating a campaign it is the effect the campaign has had upon the target group(s) and not the general public which is critical.

Specification and achievement of goals, aims, objectives

Campaign programmes require statements of goals, aims and objectives, a view unequivocally shared by Patsy Hutchinson and John Kirby of Sheffield City Polytechnic Library:

> 'It is essential to have clear objectives . . . It is important that objectives are agreed with and backed by senior management and that all staff are aware of them.'[8]

Without such statements the campaign lacks direction or has only a vague sense of direction, it becomes difficult if not impossible to plan successfully and it is not possible to satisfactorily evaluate the campaign as it lacks the measures and benchmarks which may be used for assessment.

To the pedant, distinctions may be made between goals, aims and objectives but for our purposes here, they are generally used collectively. What is important is that they should be realistic, appropriate and, in the case of objectives, measurable. Realistic and appropriate, because of the resource constraints imposed on the campaign and what might be reasonable to achieve. Measurable, so that the evaluation process may reveal the relative success of the campaign. What is often under-estimated is the value of evaluating the possible likelihood of campaign success even before it has commenced, and this may be done subjectively by comparing expectations of what is to be achieved with the plans to achieve them. Some campaigns are doomed to failure even before they start because of over-ambitious objectives and under-resourced plans.

As we shall see later, because of the nature of the communications process, campaign goals, aims and objectives may relate to a range of possible aspects — from raising levels of awareness, to changing people's perceptions, to encouraging them to take some form of action such as attending an event or joining a library. For example, in creating an identity for Sheffield City Polytechnic Library,[9] the aims related to providing information, advertising services, creating a positive attitude, and creating a sense of corporate identity in the five constituent libraries while retaining each library's individuality. Hampshire County Library when launching 'Hantsline' stated their main objective as:

> To increase public awareness of the range and diversity of information available freely through the public library network and thus contribute to the social, educational, commercial, and democratic well-being of the County.[10]

This might be better referred to as an aim rather than an objective but, whatever the term used, it clearly lays importance on awareness generation. Further elements of their aims included the wish to promote Hampshire locally and nationally as a major information provider and to present a corporate image to users.

This, then, gives some idea of what constitutes a promotional campaign. But what of the communications process which is set in train at the launch of a campaign programme and on which the results are so dependent?

CAMPAIGN DESIGN, COMMUNICATIONS AND ACTION

Successful promotional campaigns have two broad areas of effect, a communications effect and a sales or action effect.[11] A campaign may create such communications effects as increasing levels of awareness and engendering a particular image or impression as well as leading to such actions as increasing library membership, the giving of funds and encouraging more people to take part in an event. Campaign objectives (and their evaluation) may be directed at either or both of these areas. A greater appreciation of the communications process giving rise to these effects will lead to a greater understanding of the evaluation process.

Numerous attempts have been made to model communications, most of which have many features in common but tend to differ with regard to the complexity and detail proposed. Examples may be found in Schramm,[12] Engel et al,[13] Rothschild[14] and Kotler.[15] Stated explicitly in some and only implied in other models is the influence communications have on subsequent behaviour. In the business world, the behaviour which is ultimately sought is invariably a sale although many other actions, perceptions, and attitude changes could be equally valid. In relation to library services the action may well be payment for a service or membership and use of a library and, although library users may not normally be viewed as buyers, subscribers to, users of and participators in library services may be considered to behave in ways similar to 'conventional' buyers and users of commercial products and services. Recognition of the 'buying' process is valuable in this context: it has considerable impact on the selection of campaign objectives, campaign design and implementation, and campaign evaluation. Not only, then, are models of the communications process of interest but so too are models of 'buyer behaviour', if an understanding of promotional campaigns and their evaluation is to be fully embraced.

Figure 1 attempts to combine communication and action/buyer effects and to illustrate the principal elements in the total process. Broadly speaking, the model displays five major aspects. First, the environment and context in which the communication and action takes place. This has been numbered 1 on the figure. Second, the major parties involved, namely: the source or original sender of the communication [2i]; the receivers of the communication [2ii] (who might also transmit information to others [2iv] and who may be either part of the target audience or part of the non-targeted audience); and those who choose to take action or remain inactive [2iii], whether or not they are the original receivers of the information. Third, the main communication 'tools'; the message or content [3i] and the media which transmit the communication [3ii]. Fourth, the encoding [4i] and decoding [4ii] process which takes place as the sender determines the message to be sent and the receiver attempts to translate the meanings of that message. In both situations, interference, barriers to the communication

FIGURE 1: Process of Communication and Action.

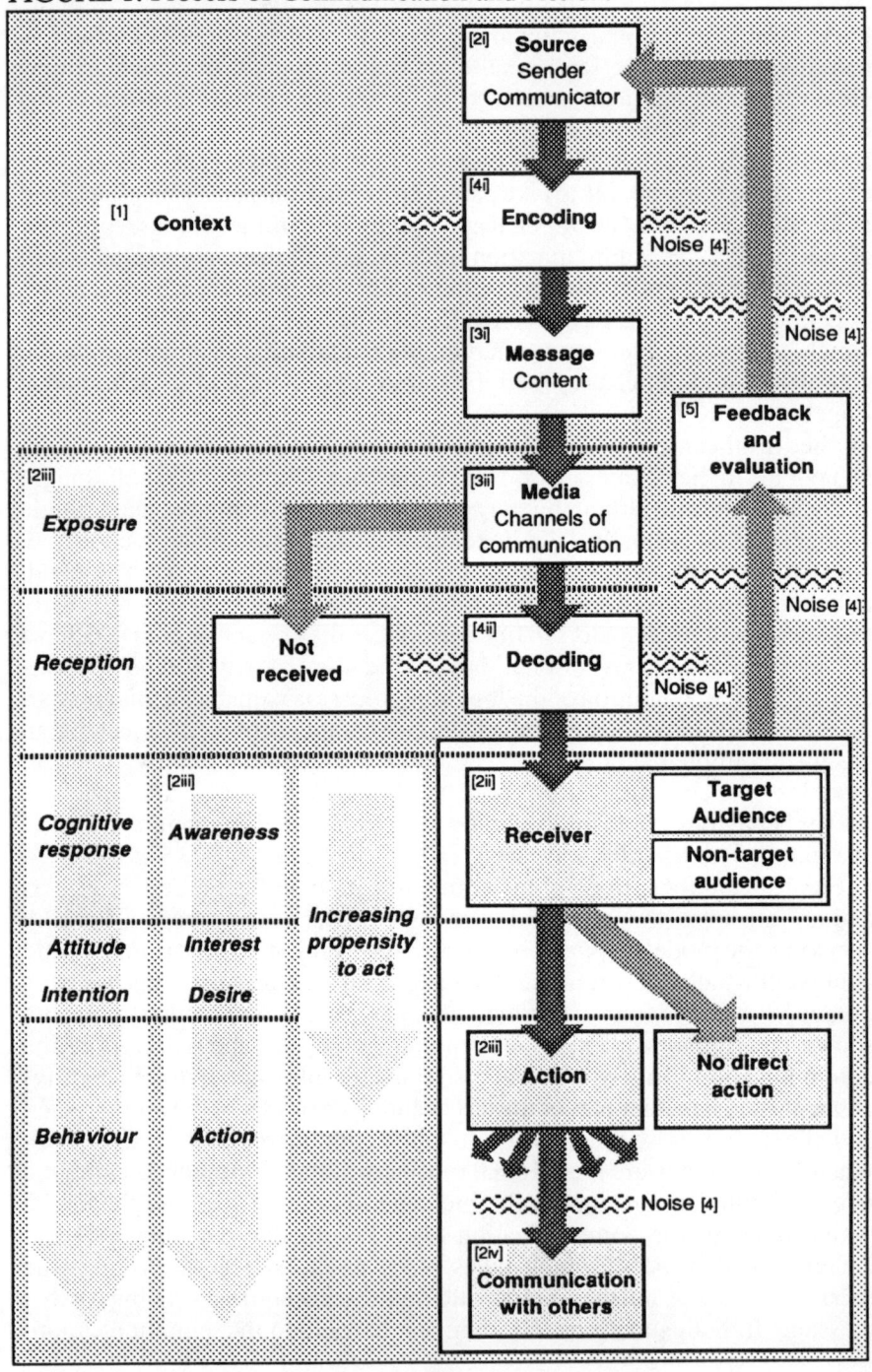

or 'noise' [4] occurs, which may give rise to inaccurate transmission and reception of the intended communication. Fifth, the feedback and evaluation process [5].

Context [1]

Factors in the environment which are frequently outside the control of the initiator of the communication will affect the success of a campaign. In particular, it should be noted that communications do not take place in a vacuum and that things which are currently occurring and things which have gone before will have an impact on the reception and credibility of the message. For example, people's general image of libraries, library services and librarians will affect their perception of any new messages received. The BBC series of comedy programmes, *Sorry,* have done little to enhance the image of today's librarians.

The context of a campaign may be very much more immediate and direct. If a poster is placed on a wall, its surroundings will affect its impact. Some local authorities include promotional material with the rates bills. If that promotional material is asking for the payment of a subscription, its inclusion with a rates demand may not represent good timing.

Parties Involved — Sender [2i], Receivers [2ii], Actors [2iii]

Source Credibility

The success or otherwise of a campaign has just as much to do with the people involved as it has to do with the message. One potential difficulty arises out of the 'source credibility' of the sender. The believability and impact of a message is considerably affected by the perceptions held of the sender by the receivers of that message. This is a particular problem if negative feelings are held by the target audience who, despite the fact that other elements of the campaign are perfectly acceptable, may not react in a way the campaign is seeking to encourage. Evaluation of source credibility even before the beginning of a campaign can be very worthwhile. By making use of a spokesperson or group which the target audience is known to respect, source credibility can be significantly improved.

Targeting

Arguments on the grounds of economy, efficiency and effectiveness emphasise the need to target campaigns at one or more specified audiences rather than the world at large or the 'general public'. The messages and the media used will need to be carefully selected for appropriateness for each target and a campaign's effectiveness will most certainly be affected by these factors. Despite targeting efforts, however, members of a non-targeted audience will frequently receive the message. This, in itself, need be no bad thing except in sensitive situations, although where it occurs it may imply the use of the wrong media.

The Decision-making Unit

Intuitively appreciated by many but ignored by others is the need to recognise what some grandiosely refer to as the Decision Making Unit or Group, the DMU.[16] Within the target audience decisions to act will be influenced or otherwise affected by many others. Typically, the DMU, whether organised formally or informally, may consist of an initiator, influencers, decider, buyer and users.

This is ably illustrated when consideration is given to the way in which some children join libraries. The influencers may be parents, school teachers, other children; the initiator and decider could be the child or parent; the buyer, or in this case the person who completes the membership form, might be the mother or father; and the user, of course, is the child. Even though a campaign may have as an objective increasing child membership to a specified level, the campaign itself may comprise promotions aimed at any or all groups identified in the DMU. The targeting only of children may have limited success.

Importantly, the DMU concept emphasises that whatever the general description of the target audience, different approaches and messages may be needed for different members of the DMU within the target. Promotions for children will be different from those aimed at parents, which may be different from those aimed at teachers. Evaluation of a campaign thus requires consideration of target audiences, DMUs, and the quality of message and media for each.

The Buying/Action Process — the hierarchy of effects

Of particular note in the 'buying process' are the typical stages people go through over a period of time (sometimes short, sometimes long), and which many researchers have attempted to model. The framework most frequently adopted is that of a 'hierarchy of effects', which commences with initial awareness of a product or service to eventual action in terms of purchase/repurchase and use.[17,18,19] The terms used by different researchers may differ but the hierarchical processes proposed are similar. (It should be noted that there are those who criticise the approach — usually on the grounds of over-simplification, e.g. Haskins,[20] Palda.[21])

Figure 1 illustrates the process most simply by reference to the movement of the audience from Awareness to Interest to Desire and finally to Action (AIDA). Through this process, the audience is *exposed* to the communication, it is *received* and there is a *cognitive response* as the communication is decoded. *Attitudes* are formed as a precursor to the *intention* to act and, if the campaign is successful, there is appropriate *behaviour* in the form of purchase, use or communication with others (word of mouth).[22]

Word of mouth is invariably very powerful, often under-estimated and frequently ignored by campaign planners. Yet an appreciation of the DMU concept allows recognition of the important role of influencers who are often our peers and those whose views we respect. Word of mouth, in a sense, is a medium of communication which often has a high level of source credibility but over which we exert little control over the quality of message relayed.

The significance of the hierarchy of effects model is that the process is one-way and that each stage has to be gone through in turn. For example, a campaign devised to incite current non-members to join a library will have little success before they are first made aware of, have interest in, and desire the benefits library membership will bring. In order to maintain library membership and use, the hierarchy of effects model may be extended to include repeat behaviour so that a campaign may be devised to encourage the existing users to continue or even increase their use of the services. To this end, the campaign may concentrate on reminding people about library services and the reassertion of values and benefits to the user target audience.

From the perspective of campaign evaluation, consideration has to be given to campaign objectives and appropriate measures for each of the stages in the 'buying process'. Recall of a campaign may be suitable to measure levels of awareness, but will only vaguely imply intention to act.

Message [3i] and Media [3ii]

As suggested above, the selection of appropriate message and media will be affected first by the choice of target audience and secondly by the closer targeting within that audience of members of the decision making group. The words and imagery used will be different as will the approach adopted to convey those messages through posters, leaflets, local radio, visits and face-to-face contact, telephone, etc. Even entrance areas, signs, library layouts and so on will have their effect.

The quality of message may be evaluated before a campaign commences as well as during or after its completion and the media chosen for transmission of the message can be evaluated in terms of its ability to 'reach' the target audience, the 'frequency' with which the message is received and its appropriateness for the target. Collectively, the 'impact' of a particular campaign may be assessed. If too weak, a campaign may not achieve its objectives because it is unable to create enough impact.

Noise [4], Encoding [4i] and Decoding [4ii]

Once the sender of the communication has determined the message to be transmitted, that message needs to be put into a form suitable for both the media and the receivers. In this translation process much can go wrong and the message transmitted may not be the same as that intended. A similar problem occurs in the decoding process, in which the message received is translated in terms understandable to the receiver. For the message to be effective, the sender's encoding process must mesh with the receiver's decoding process.[23] Noise [4] represents distortion or even lack of message reception by the target audience and may result in unintended meanings being ascribed to the communication.

Evaluation is vital if we are to be sure that our campaign messages have been received by the right people and that the intended meanings have been conveyed with sufficient impact. Care has to be taken, however, because the noise which occurs in transmission/reception also occurs in the feedback process, which seeks to investigate and understand the nature of the communication between sender and receiver.

Feedback and Evaluation [5]

As this is a principal theme of this chapter, it should be emphasised that feedback and evaluation should be an important and integral part of the communications (and therefore campaign planning) process. Of equal importance is the recognition based on the foregoing discussion that such evaluation does not take place only at the end of a campaign. Any one or more of the elements and variables may affect the quality of a campaign's eventual outcome and, thus, its perceived success or failure. A campaign design which does not take into account the effects and impact of the communications variables must be considered suspect even before it has been implemented. It is therefore possible to start the evaluation process (as well it should) well before the campaign commences.

The context, the source, the message, the media, the receivers, the hierarchy of effects leading to action, the noise in the system are all elements worthy of consideration in campaign design and, correspondingly, they are all elements worthy of note in the evaluation process.

VALUE FOR MONEY — ECONOMY, EFFICIENCY AND EFFECTIVENESS

There is ever increasing concern, and legitimately so, that library campaign programmes as well as other public expenditure should be seen to be value for money. As David Yorke, points out when commenting on 'The quality of library services',

> 'The emotive phrase 'value for money' has become commonplace in most of the town halls in the UK.'

Some years ago a report was presented to the British Library Research and Development Department concerning a special campaign research project involving direct mail promotions.[25] Having spent over £500 in a campaign to recruit new library users, the project was brought to a close when only two new members were believed to be recruited as a direct result of the campaign's activities. In evaluating the campaign, the researchers understandably believed that £500 to recruit two new library members did not represent value for money. In the words of the researchers, 'The total cost in relation to the impact (less than 1%) cannot be justified.' This seems entirely reasonable and the post-testing evaluation process was quite sophisticated compared to that which was currently taking place within libraries. However, if the proposed campaign had been evaluated before its implementation as has been emphasised throughout this chapter, and with greater consideration of the communication and action process, the costs of evaluation could have been reduced and a better campaign may have been devised which did deliver value for money.

Butt and Palmer[26] suggest that value for money consists of three basic elements, each of which justifies careful evaluation: *Economy, Efficiency, and Effectiveness*. Economy, they maintain, is the practice by management of the virtues of thrift and good housekeeping. Economical operations are those in which resources are acquired in appropriate qualities and quantities at lowest cost. Efficiency is a measure of the extent to which greatest output is gained from the resources used or else the extent to which the level of resources used to achieve a given output is minimised. This dual aspect of efficiency highlights the notions of under and over promotion. In developing and implementing a promotional campaign it is usual to worry about whether success will be achieved. But, specifically from an efficiency point of view, exceeding campaign expectations is no better than failing to meet them. Effectiveness, on the other hand, is concerned with the extent to which the activities selected for a campaign are the most suitable to achieve the results desired. Effectiveness is about doing the right things, efficiency is doing things right. As the Chartered Institute of Public Finance and Accountancy (CIPFA) have stated in their Standards:

> 'Economy and efficiency in the execution of programmes are of small consequence if the programmes are not meeting (their) objectives and no assessment of value for money is complete without regard to effectiveness.'[27]

Effects

Studies of advertising and promotions have led to a number of questions being raised about the effects generated through promotional campaigns. Again, a brief recognition of some of these may lead to a better understanding of campaign design and evaluation.

(a) Cumulative effect — there are positive gains derived from the synergistic effect of undertaking a number of promotional activities. Each element of the promotion, each advertisement placed, improves the overall effectiveness of the campaign.

(b) Lagged effects — it is not uncommon to find that there is a delay between the transmission of a message and consequent action. Sometimes this delay might be quite long, depending upon such things as the type of promotion carried out, the media used and the nature of the message.

(c) Decay — unless promotions are repeated or reinforced, their effect diminishes over time.

(d) Diminishing returns — a point is reached after which promotional effectiveness begins to diminish. Each promotional activitiy may be effective, but at a reducing rate. In rare cases this can lead to negative results if the promotion is 'overdone'.

(e) Minimum threshold — this is linked to the cumulative effects of promotions and suggests that unless a minimum level of promotion is carried out little or no effect is seen.

(f) Fitness for purpose – some types of promotion are better than others in fulfilling campaign objectives. Advertising is very good at raising levels of awareness whereas the use of telephones and face-to-face promotions can be very effective at getting people to do things. A mix of promotions becomes very useful in moving people through the various stages of the hierarchy of effects process, ultimately leading to action.

(g) Media effects — depending upon the target audience to be reached and the promotional objective to be met, some media are more effective than others. They are capable of reaching more of the target and in such a way as to better achieve the objectives set. There are also positioning effects which refer to the timing and placing of promotions within the media. For example, a particular promotion may be most effective if placed on local commercial radio, scheduled to be heard at a particular time in a programme concerning a particular topic and to coincide with a particular event, or an advertisement may be best placed in a certain position within a magazine.

(h) Synergy with other marketing elements — promotions are only one part of the range of marketing activities. The extent to which all these activities complement each other will have an impact on their overall effectiveness. At its simplest, all the promotional effort in the world will be of little consequence if the product or service being promoted is not what people want, or can afford, or is not made available to them at the right time and in the right place.

By paying attention to these effects in evaluating campaigns, the reasons for success or failure may become more apparent and more effective campaigns may be devised.

TECHNIQUES OF EVALUATION

Techniques and approaches to campaign evaluation take many forms because of the nature of what is to be evaluated and the variety of goals, aims and objectives which may be set for the campaign. The evaluation may be of a specific element or elements such as a particular image, message or advertisement, or may be of the total effect of the campaign in its entirety. It may concern itself with communication or action effects and may begin before the start of the campaign, during the period in which it is running or after its completion. The form the evaluation may take could be qualitative or quantitative and may be anything from highly subjective to highly objective. These issues are not least affected by the resources made available for the evaluation process. Depending on these resources, the evaluation could be very comprehensive or may seek answers only to limited questions and, given the resource implications, it would be improper to suggest an ideal scale of operations. Perhaps the advice to be given is that at least *some* form of evaluation should be attempted, within what is reasonable and practical under prevailing circumstances.

What follows is some indication of what does take place in industry and what could be done in libraries. The degree of popularity of each evaluation approach varies from user to user and from situation to situation. Jobber and Kilbride[28] in a survey of UK advertising agencies discovered a considerable variation in the sophistication of techniques used. Although each evaluation approach has its own benefits and drawbacks it is not the place here to explore them in detail. The intention is to identify possible approaches rather than debate their relative merits and demerits (for example, see Lovell, *et al*,[29] Sampson and Hooper[30] and Mostyn[31]) In each case, if carried out by experienced practitioners, the results are more likely to be valid, accurate and reliable. However, through practice and judicious use of the methods suggested, librarians will be able to build up this experience for themselves.

Based on an understanding of the communication and action process, a range of aspects or areas of evaluation may be identified. An outline of some of the significant ones is presented in Table 1. Each aspect is considered with regard to the stage in the campaign when it is best evaluated (but this is not to suggest that evaluation could not take place at other stages). Examples are given of suitable evaluation approaches in each case and these are more fully described below.

The list of techniques presented here does not attempt to be comprehensive but has been selected to be illustrative of the range available. Some are more novel than others and some may even be surprising. Some have inherited the phrase 'quick and dirty methods' because of their lack of sophistication and only relative accuracy. Some will be beyond the scope of many library campaigns.

	STAGE IN THE CAMPAIGN			EXAMPLES OF EVALUATION APPROACHES
	BEFORE LAUNCH PRE-TEST	DURING CAMPAIGN DURING TEST	AFTER CAMPAIGN POST-TEST	
ASPECTS TO BE EVALUATED	CAMPAIGN RESOURCES eg: Facilities, Finance/Budget, Manpower, Time			Assessment against objectives set for campaign EXPERT OPINION VICARIOUS EXPERIENCE PAST RECORDS
	TARGETING AND DECISION MAKING UNIT DECISIONS			EXPERT OPINION VICARIOUS EXPERIENCE PAST RECORDS
	CAMPAIGN MANAGEMENT i.e.: planning	CAMPAIGN MANAGEMENT		EXPERT OPINION CRITICAL REVIEW
	SOURCE CREDIBILITY CONTEXT			ATTITUDE SURVEY – QUESTIONNAIRE DISCUSSION GROUPS RECORDS
	MEDIA Selection Scheduling Timing Frequency Reach Positioning		MEDIA REVIEW	MEDIA ANALYSIS eg: cost effectiveness audience reached recall tests
	MESSAGE, IMAGE, DESIGN			TARGET AUDIENCE – DIRECT RATING: RECOGNITION AND RECALL TESTS TRACKING STUDIES LABORATORY TESTS DISCUSSION GROUPS IN-DEPTH INTERVIEWS
	PRE-CAMPAIGN AWARENESS, ATTITUDES AND BEHAVIOUR	CAMPAIGN AWARENESS AND UNDERSTANDING, ATTITUDE CHANGES, BEHAVIOUR CHANGES		QUESTIONNAIRE SURVEY PAST RECORDS DISCUSSION GROUPS IN-DEPTH INTERVIEWS DIRECT RESPONSE AREA TESTS
	PROMOTIONAL MIX			Appropriate balance and synergy EXPERT OPINION PAST RECORDS
			TOTAL CAMPAIGN REVIEW	Assessment against objectives set for campaign RECORDS REVIEW OF OTHER EVALUATION

TABLE 1: Campaign Evaluation — Aspects to be considered

Techniques of Evaluation

list

Expert opinion

Before the promotional campaign is launched, one or more 'experts' may be requested to view the proposed campaign, or elements of it. Their opinions may be 'loosely' collected or they may be asked to allocate ratings against specified criteria. The method relies on subjective appraisal but nevertheless this can be of value, particularly if the evaluators are experienced. Alternative designs and messages may also be evaluated through this process. A specially designed rating sheet may be used as illustrated in Table 2, this one is for the evaluation of advertisements. A new sheet would be used for each advertisement tested and for each evaluator. The total scores and the ratings against each criterion can be compared and, given the objectives set, a decision can be made about the quality of the advertisements being tested. The higher the scores, the better the advertisement.

TABLE 2: *Example of rating sheet*

RATING SHEET

		Score out of 20
Attention/Impact	How well does the ad. catch the readers attention?	—
Creative Strength	How well is the ad. designed, does it appeal to the target reader?	—
Read-through strength	How well does the ad. lead the reader to read further? Is the ad interesting?	—
Cognitive Strength	How clear is the central message or benefit?	—
Affective Strength	How effective is the particular appeal? Is the ad. believeable?	—
Behavioural Strength	How well does the ad. suggest follow-through action?	—
	TOTAL	

Target audience opinion — direct ratings

This method is identical to the above but has the distinct advantage that one or more sample groups from the campaign's target audience(s) are selected to complete the evaluation sheets. Instead of relying on expert opinion, the information is collected 'straight from the horses mouth'.

Discussion Groups

One, two or more groups of, perhaps, five to eight people representing members of the target audience are selected to discuss aspects of the campaign under the guidance of a group leader. The groups are allowed freely to discuss issues they consider pertinent rather than being asked a series of direct questions. It is the group leader's responsibility to ensure that the groups address relevant issues without being too directive or interrogative. Used particularly as a pre-testing method, the group discussion can reveal important findings concerning the campaign which may lead, for example, to significant changes to proposed messages and creative treatments.

In-depth Interviews

Just as the group discussion method may be used to elicit thoughts, ideas, feelings and attitudes held about a previous, existing or proposed campaign so too can the in-depth interview. On a one-to-one basis the evaluator can ask a series of questions of a sample of the target audience. The degree of structure within such interviews varies but opportunity should always be given for the respondents to express their own views, some of which the evaluator may not have previously considered. This method should not be confused with face-to-face questionnaire surveys although they may share the use of some direct measures such as attitude scaling.

Questionnaire Surveys

Detailed questionnaires are produced and are administered by the evaluators on face-to-face, telephone or postal bases. Care is taken to ensure that each respondent in the sample is treated in the same way so that results may be compared. Many more respondents may be questioned in this way than in the previous approaches and use may be made of attitude measures as part of the questionnaire. The survey may make use of one of a number of the approaches described below.

Recognition and Recall Tests

These may be used at all stages in a promotional campaign and can take a number of forms. In the case of printed material (e.g.: advertisements, leaflets, posters), the term 'portfolio test' is often used because the evaluator makes use of a folder to display examples of the promotion. If used as a pre-test, a sample of people from the target audience will be shown the promotional material and asked what they remember. Alternative designs and messages may be tested in this way and, if desired, comparisons with 'competitor' promotions can be made. Questions can be asked not only of what is remembered but also of what the respondents think and feel about what they have seen.

If these tests are used during the campaign or after it has finished, a number of options are possible. Unaided recall questions may be asked without showing examples of the promotions. If examples are shown then the test becomes one of recognition. If part of the promotional material is shown, say part of a leaflet, this is a form of aided recall. In each case, the amount respondents remember, the degree of accuracy of their recall and the attitudes they hold about the subject of the promotions become measures of the potential effectiveness of the campaign material. Tracking studies may use such recognition, recall and attitude measures. The term 'tracking' is simply used to describe before, during and after measurements so that the progress of a campaign may be plotted: the amount of change which takes place being ascribed to the effectiveness of the campaign (other things being equal).

The easiest measure which may be used in these tests is that of awareness. That is to say, is the respondent aware of the promotion or not; is the advertisement or message remembered? More sophisticated are the measures of attitudes which typically make use of one or more attitude scaling approaches. Examples of these can be found in many texts on consumer behaviour and consumer and market research, e.g.: Chisnall,[32] Engel et al,[33] Oppenheim[34] and Tull and Hawkins.[35]

'Laboratory' Tests

These tests make use of a variety of testing equipment, some of which are described below. They are of particular use in pre-testing promotional material.

Tachistoscope — this is a piece of equipment which flashes a visual display of the promotional material very quickly. The speed of the flash can be adjusted, sometimes from as little as one hundredth of a second, so that an assessment of the relative impact of, say, an advertisement or an element of an advertisement can be made. More simply, a slide projector may be used or even a blank piece of paper to cover over the item of promotion under test. Respondents are briefly shown the visual for a set period of time and asked to describe what has been seen. The longer the average period needed before the display is intelligible the less the immediate impact it has. The method may be used to test the relative legibility and efficiency of different type faces and material, presentations of logos, slogans and layouts, and can help to find out which elements take the most time to be noticed and remembered.

Eye movement camera — the camera tracks and records eye movement as the viewer scans the promotional material being evaluated. It can be seen from the visual record which elements were popular and attracted attention and which went relatively unseen. If key areas go unnoticed in this way the material may need re-designing.

Pupil response — a camera records changes in pupil size during the viewing of promotional material. The greater the increase in pupil size, which is an autonomic response occurring when we like things we see, the greater the favourable reaction caused by the material being viewed.

So far, the approaches presented above have broadly related to the communications effects of a campaign or part of a campaign. The following methods tend to be more concerned, but not necessarily totally so, with the behavioural effects of a campaign giving rise to some form of action taking place.

Direct response and coupon returns

Some advertisements or leaflets require a direct response, such as in the case of direct mail advertisements, or include a response card or coupon return. These approaches can be used as measures of effectiveness and efficiency. The greater the response or number of coupons returned, the more effective the promotion has been. Different media may be tested in this way and an assessment made of their efficiency by measuring costs against the number of replies received. It is not uncommon to test different magazines and newspapers in this way by having a different code number on the advertisement appearing in each publication.

Area Tests and Split Runs

A carefully selected area rather than the whole catchment may be used to test a campaign. If all is well the campaign may be fully launched or else the experiences of the test may suggest that certain changes should be made before the launch goes ahead. In a similar way, more than one area could be selected for test purposes and each could be used for a modified version of the campaign, the most effective approach being selected for full launch. This type of evaluation procedure may be used equally well to test both communication and action effects of campaigns.

Some sophisticated models have been used in this context such as AMTES, the Area Test Evaluation System,[36] which makes use of market experimentation and econometric analysis to develop a statistical model of a given market place. AMTES is thus able to allow statistically for the effects of factors other than the promotional campaign when assessing its effectiveness. Short of such complex approaches, other factors which may affect the outcome of a campaign may be allowed for by using a commonsense check that anything which may have a significant effect on the campaign either did not change too much during the campaign period or else is taken into account when assessing the results.

Records

This is a catch-all heading to emphasise the need to make use of past records which are kept of library membership, attendances, use of particular services, etc. Where such records are not kept or are not kept in such a way as to be easily obtainable, this situation should be remedied. Any campaigns which are undertaken in the future should be carefully recorded with regard to campaign activities, timings, use of resources and measures of effects. When evaluating current campaigns, comparison should be made with past records and results noted. Future campaigns may be further assessed against past results. Particular promotions may prove to be more effective than others and these should be capitalised on. If a campaign has action-related objectives such as increasing the use of a service, records of use both before and after the campaign will give a direct measure of success.

Media analysis

Data may be obtained either from media owners (publishers, radio and TV stations, etc.) or from publications like *British Rate And Data* (BRAD) and the *National Readership Survey* (NRS) which enable evaluation of possible media effectiveness, efficiency and economy. Circulation, readership, listening and viewing figures can be compared against cost so that an assessment can be made of possible media alternatives. A typical measure would be cost per thousand of the target audience reached.

Evaluation may also be made of such things as the scheduling, timing, frequency and positioning of promotions — bearing in mind some of the effects described earlier. These types of assessment are the stock in trade of campaign and media planners in industry.

Vicarious experience

Much promotional work is being conducted throughout the library service. Some of this work is published, some goes unnoticed. A great deal could be learned by sharing and comparing experiences and data with other libraries. Collectively, the evaluation of library promotional activities throughout the country and overseas could do much to improve the effectiveness of future campaigns and there is much to learn from the private, commercial sector who have been involved in evaluating and improving campaign performance for many years. The wheel does not have to be re-invented.

Furthermore, outside agencies may be used in researching, collecting, collating and evaluating information. They may even be used in the design of the campaign itself. Obviously, there are professionals, but there may be resource constraints on their use. If used conscientiously, students and staff in higher business education may be a satisfactory alternative.

If used wisely, these techniques, and perhaps a number of others not presented here, can provide invaluable tools for the analysis and evaluation of a campaign programme.

SUMMARY

This chapter has tried to emphasise the need for campaign evaluation and, in attempting to foster greater understanding, has outlined some significant aspects of the communication and action process. The descriptions have been necessarily brief and the reader is encouraged to make use of the many texts available on the relevant topics.

Judicious use of evaluation has been shown, over and over again, to improve campaign economy, efficiency and effectiveness, not just for present campaigns but, through accumulated knowledge and experience, those of the future. Campaign evaluation takes many and varied forms and these should be selected on grounds of suitability. With consideration of practical issues, such evaluation may not be entirely objective and trustworthy: compromises do have to be made, but this should not discourage librarians from evaluating. Rather, it should give rise to more careful and considered application.

Complementary techniques should be used for assessing campaigns in whole or in part, whether as pre-, during or post- tests and these need to be matched against the resources available. Relatively speaking, pre-testing can be used with effect without incurring too great a cost and with the corresponding advantage that modifications can be made to the campaign before it is allowed to proceed.

If nothing succeeds like success then the evaluation process is not an optional extra. And it is most certainly not an expensive luxury. Evaluation helps increase the chances of success and delivers the measures which may be used to prove it. It creates a greater understanding of campaign planning and encourages appropriate campaign modification. It may be used to secure greater resources for future activity and it may even assist in the problem of resource allocation by highlighting areas of waste:

> 'Evaluation... may not supply all the answers. But it can provide enough of them to make it an essential function for every organisation'[37]

REFERENCES

1. WOOD, D. Improving your image: How to promote a library or information service. *Aslib Proceedings,* 36 (10), 1984, 401-408.
2. CRONIN, B. From paradigm to practice: the logic of promotion. *Aslib Proceedings,* 33 (10), 1981, 383-392.
3. WHATLEY, A. The untapped market for the public library: a survey. *Library Association Record,* 80 (9), 1978, 447-449, 467.
4. CRONIN, B., From paradigm to practice: the logic of promotion. *Aslib Proceedings,* 33 (10), 1981, 383-392.
5. BERGER, P. An investigation of the relationship between public relations activities and budget allocation in public libraries. *Information Processing and Management,* 15 (4), 1979, 179-193.
6. WEISS, C. *Evaluation research: methods for assessing program effectiveness.* Englewood Cliffs, NJ: Prentice-Hall, 1972.
7. SYKES, P. *The public library in perspective.* London: Bingley, 1979.
8. HUTCHINSON, P. and KIRBY, J. Creating an identity. *Aslib Proceedings,* 33 (10), 1981, 400-404.
9. HUTCHINSON, P. and KIRBY, J. Creating an identity. *Aslib Proceedings,* 33 (10), 1981, 400-404.
10. FOX, N. Hantsline — a strategy for publicity. *Library Association Record,* 88 (2), 1986, 83-84.
11. KOTLER, P. *Marketing management — analysis, planning, implementation and control.* 6th ed. Englewood Cliffs, NJ: Prentice-Hall, 1988.
12. SCHRAMM, W. How communication works *In:* W. Schramm and D. F. Roberts, eds. *The process and effects of mass communication* .University of Illinois Press, 1971.
13. ENGEL, J.F., BLACKWELL, R.D. and MINIARD, P.W. *Consumer behaviour.* 5th ed. New York: Dryden Press, 1986.
14. ROTHSCHILD, M.L. *Marketing communications: from fundamentals to strategies.* Lexington Mass: D.C. Heath, 1987.
15. KOTLER, P. *Marketing management — analysis ,planning, implementation and control*, 6th ed. Englewood Cliffs, NJ: Prentice-Hall, 1988.

16. KOTLER, P. *Marketing management — analysis, planning, implementation and control*. 6th ed. Englewood Cliffs, NJ: Prentice-Hall, 1988.
17. STRONG, E.K. *The psychology of selling*. New York: McGraw-Hill, 1925.
18. LAVIDGE, R.J. *and* STEINER, G.A. A model for predictive measurements of advertising effectiveness. *Journal of Marketing,* 25 (6), 1961, 59-62.
19. COLLEY, R.H., *Defining advertising goals for measured advertising results*. New York: Association of National Advertisers, 1961.
20. HASKINS, J.B. Factual recall as a measure of advertising effectiveness. *Journal of Advertising Research*, 4 (1), 1964.
21. PALDA, K.S. The hypothesis of a hierarchy of effects: a partial evaluation. *Journal of Marketing Research,* 3 (1), 1966, 13-24.
22. KOTLER, P. *Marketing management — analysis, planning, implementation and control*. 6th ed. Englewood Cliffs, NJ: Prentice-Hall, 1988.
23. KOTLER, P. *Marketing management — analysis, planning, implementation and control*. 6th ed. Englewood Cliffs, NJ: Prentice-Hall, 1988.
24. YORKE, D. The quality of library services. In: B. Moores, ed., *Are they being served? Quality consciousness in service industries*. Oxford: Philip Allan, 1986.
25. CRONIN, B. *Direct mail advertising and public library use*. London: British Library, 1979. (British Library Research and Development Report No. 5539).
26. BUTT, H. *and* PALMER, R. *Value for money in the public sector*. Oxford: Basil Blackwell, 1985.
27. YORKE, D. The quality of library services. In: B. Moores, ed. *Are they being served? Quality consciousness in service industries*. Oxford: Philip Allan, 1986.
28. JOBBER, D. *and* KILBRIDE, A. How major advertising agencies evaluate TV advertising in Great Britain. *International Journal of Advertising,* 5 (3), 1986, 187-195.
29. LOVELL, M.R.C., JOHNS, S. *and* RAMPLEY, B. *Pre-testing press advertisements. In: Ten years of advertising media research*, London: The Thompson Organisation, 1972.
30. SAMPSON, P. *and* HOOPER, B. *Evaluating "Below-The-Line" Expenditure. In:Ten years of advertising media research*. London: The Thompson Organisation, 1972.
31. MOSTYN, B.J. *A handbook of motivational and attitude research techniques*. Bradford: MCB, 1978.
32. CHISNALL, P.M. *Marketing: a behavioural analysis*. 2nd ed. London: McGraw-Hill, 1985.
33. ENGEL, J.F., BLACKWELL, R.D. *and* MINIARD, P.W. *Consumer behaviour*. 5th ed. New York: Dryden Press, 1986.
34. OPPENHEIM, A.N. *Questionnaire design and attitude measurement*. London: Heinemann, 1966.
35. TULL, D.S. *and* HAWKINS, D.I. *Marketing research*, 3rd ed. New York: Macmillan, 1984.
36. BROADBENT, S. *Advertising works 1980:* London: Holt, Rinehart and Winston, 1981.
37. WEISS, C. *Evaluation research: methods for assessing program effectiveness*. Englewood Cliffs, NJ: Prentice-Hall, 1972.,

CHAPTER TEN
THE IMPORTANCE OF PUBLIC RELATIONS IN INFORMATION SERVICE ORGANIZATIONS

Bob Usherwood

> Girl: "See that building there? That's the library"
> (PAUSE)
> Girl: "If you ever want to borrow a book all you have to do is go in there and tell them which one you want and they'll let you take it home"
> Boy: "FREE?"
> Girl: "Absolutely free!"
> Boy: "Sort of makes you wonder what they're up to!"

Edward Bernays, generally regarded as the father of modern public relations has called public relations a process 'that furthers mutual understanding and co-operation between an individual, a corporation, or any organization and its various publics'.[1] The above dialogue, taken from an old Peanuts cartoon, emphasises the importance of this process for library and information service organizations; there is an obvious need to increase the awareness of materials and services offered.

For public service organizations, such as libraries, establishing that mutual understanding, mentioned by Bernays, is now a matter of survival. Public library and information services, in common with all public services, are having to withstand populist campaigns for cuts in public expenditure, whilst at the same time having to meet the challenge of the new technology and alternative and, to use the vogue phrase, more sexy forms of service delivery.

Looked at again in the harsh political and social environment of the late 1980s, the Peanuts characters demonstrate that effective library public relations is also required to allay public suspicion of public services, a suspicion and anti-public service ethos that is being encouraged by a press whose owners have media ambitions which, in some cases, run counter to the public provision of information services. Thus a *Sunday Times* 'journo' is given front page status and column inches for a misleading article entitled 'Throwing the book at public libraries'[2] — an article which was itself inspired by a speech from the Minister for Arts.

In such circumstances, skilful political public relations are required if the library and information professions are to obtain positive recognition, political, and public support, at both the national and local level. Research in America has demonstrated that those libraries which engage in public relations activities do show a higher level of support, measured in terms of budget allocation, as compared with those which do not.[3] At all levels of government the ground must be prepared to facilitate effective contact between the library profession and legislators.[4]

The information professions can no longer afford to regard public relations as a fringe activity, but must look on it as a management function 'based on the assumption that public opinion matters'.[5] Public opinion matters because in the final analysis the well being of the library, like that of any organization, may depend on the goodwill of all, or at least some, of the groups and individuals that make up its publics. To communicate effectively the nature of an organization is a management function; it is also a fair description of good public relations practice.

It is the intention of this contribution to adopt a practical approach so we will not spend time on academic definitions of what is public relations, what is marketing, what is advertising and the rest. There are real and important differences but they need not detain us here. Public relations, marketing, and entrepreneurial skills have of late become buzz words amongst library and information professionals, and this has sometimes led people to adopt the techniques of product and profit oriented organizations in an undiscriminating fashion. Whilst there is much that can be learnt from these areas, there is also a danger that promotional communications by library organizations will fail, unless account is taken of the special factors involved when promoting services, in particular, non profit services. To quote a leading exponent in the field, William Novelli, 'persuading the public to buy a particular product . . . is a tough competitive job. But marketing social services (which usually means social *change*) is even more complex.'[6]

There are significant differences between products and services that need to be considered when planning promotional communications. For instance, it is much more difficult for a client to evaluate a service in advance, than it is for a consumer to evaluate a product prior to purchase. We can, for example, be reasonably sure that the toothpaste or washing powder that we buy this week will be much the same as the one we bought last week, if we stay with the same brand. The client however is not able to be so confident about the quality, or value, of an information service until he or she has used it, often in quite particular circumstances. Thus the consumer of such services will tend to make prior judgements on the basis of what he or she sees, or hears from other people, or by what he or she experiences on entering the library or information unit. Important factors will be such things as the atmosphere of the library and the attentiveness of the staff.

In addition, the manager of a service organization has a much greater problem of quality control, he or she has to deal with people as well as machines. Human beings are much more difficult to manage, to standardise or package than machines. To overcome this problem some commercial service organizations have in fact tried to 'package' and standardise their staff and service. For example, a McDonalds fast food establishment looks (and tastes!) much the same in any part of the world, likewise a Holiday Inn.

Staff training, especially perhaps in interpersonal skills, will probably do as much to help a library project a positive image as some of the more glamorous PR activities. In Sheffield we have, over the years, developed a training programme on interpersonal skills called 'Face to Face'. This has proved of value for staff working in all types of library and information unit. An 'on site' version is available for libraries' own in house training — but there is no need to go into detail here. Suffice it to say, that it is a management responsibility to ensure that every member of a library's staff takes care to project a positive image, and that staff make sure that their actions do not harm the reputation of the service.

Even in the age of electronic information services, no, perhaps *especially* in the age of electronic information, the status and reputation of library and information services depend, not so much on their adoption of hardware and software, but on the quality of their liveware. Ken Dowlin, a co-founder of the Electronic Library Association, has expressed the view that a major challenge for the profession is keeping libraries in touch with the community.[7] In 1986, in an interesting advertising campaign, one of the big five banks emphasised the importance of personnel and personal service in the age of automated banking. In a series of television commercials potential clients were shown lost in the labyrinths of an electronic system. In one advertisement, as the data overwhelms her, a young woman screams "I just want to talk to someone". Library clients too require personal service.

As we have seen, it is more difficult to control the quality of a service than that of a product; further it is also more difficult to manage the demand for services. Manufacturers of products can identify and use slack times to produce goods for peak periods of demand. It is much more problematic to do this for services. If we look at the commercial sector, we can observe how many service promotions are, in fact, about getting people to change their patterns of behaviour, for instance through cheap off peak travel or holiday bookings. It is difficult to see how libraries might adopt this technique, although I understand that one American hospital encouraged patients to opt for weekend surgery, when 'patient count' was low, by advertising that patients operated on at the weekend would be entered in a prize draw for a sea cruise for two.

In fact, communicating so that people change their behaviour patterns is one of the most difficult of persuasive techniques, yet many campaigns by public service organizations attempt to do just that. For instance, we try and persuade non users to become library users. Neither can, nor should, libraries use the price cut technique (be it cheap holidays or cut price shares) to encourage use or votes. There are however non monetary 'costs' for library users which it is in our power to cut — for instance the cost of bureaucratic joining procedures, or the cost of belligerent members of staff, or the insensitive labelling of catalogues or sections of stock. While on the subject of money it is necessary to note the obvious, that is that most public service organizations have inadequate budgets for public relations activities.

Publicly-funded library and information services, in common with much of the public sector, can also have additional problems in enlisting support. For instance, the benefits for the individual may be perceived as low and, in some cases, those who pay for the service may feel that they do not want it. This is perhaps a particular difficulty in the Thatcherite eighties when voters are, apparently, more concerned about their own wallets than about (say) services in support of disadvantaged groups, the arts or access to information for all. Neil Kinnock's Party Political Broadcasts were technically excellent, good enough for Senator Biden, but not effective enough where it mattered most — at the ballot box.

The differences between product and service organizations, in particular, public service organizations can then make our public relations tasks that bit more difficult. Public relations in service organizations is not simply concerned with selling the service, it has financial, political, industrial, corporate, community and other dimensions. Obviously public relations communications have to be related to the objectives of the library and its parent organization. As Greta Renborg writes:

> 'Before the objectives of a library's PR can be defined, it is necessary to define the objectives of the very library for which the PR work shall be accomplished. This process can be illustrated as:
>
> Objectives of library → Objectives of library public relations.'[8]

The discussion of library objectives, or the lack of them, would take up far more space than is available, but it is clear that specific circumstances should produce their own objectives. That having been established, it is possible to identify some generally applicable functions of library public relations. A useful guide to these can be found in a valuable statement produced for the Public Libraries Research Group. This posits four major aims:

1. To establish and maintain mutual understanding between a library and its publics.
2. To influence favourably public and governmental attitudes and opinions regarding libraries.
3. To increase the general awareness of services provided by libraries.
4. To build confidence in the services provided by libraries.

The value of confidence in an information service can be exemplified by reference to British television; when moments of national drama such as elections, royal weddings and football Cup finals are shown by both the BBC and ITV, most viewers will watch the BBC coverage. The audience has confidence in the BBC, which is perhaps the most respected broadcasting authority in the world. This confidence, or authority (in the sense that the BBC is a respected authority), factor has been described as 'marketing's magic ingredient'. Of course having gained the confidence of groups and individuals it is necessary to keep it, and from time to time it is useful to reassure them that they have made the right decision. PR can play a part in confirming as well as developing or changing attitudes.

Attitudes to libraries and reading have been found to be one of the most important factors affecting the use and non use of libraries. The Hillingdon project, carried out in the early seventies, attempted to measure attitudes to public libraries by use of a Likert scale. The work, which is fully documented in *The effective library*,[9] quite clearly demonstrated that community attitudes can be a very real barrier to library effectiveness.

Public relations practitioners have identified four types of negative attitudes that are held about organizations or services: (i) Hostility, (ii) Prejudice, (iii) Apathy, (iv) Ignorance. One of the jobs of PR in service, or any other type of organization, is to eliminate the negative and accentuate the positive, or in this case, transform negative attitudes into positive ones — so that hostility becomes sympathy, prejudice becomes acceptance, apathy becomes interest and ignorance becomes knowledge. Such a transformation will not be achieved overnight and neither will it happen without a significant amount of prior investigation, or what is termed a PR or communications audit. Such an audit would need a chapter to itself, and as I have gone into greater detail elsewhere,[10] it is, for the purposes of this contribution, taken as a 'given'.

Quite obviously the public for, and of, library and information services is not a single homogeneous one but rather a collection of a number of different groups and individuals. Each library will have special internal and external publics with whom it wants to communicate; for public relations communications to be most effective these need to be subdivided further. For example, in the case of staff one can identify a number of discrete groups and interests. Not only are there professional and para-professional workers but a whole range of specialisms and interests within those categories. External groups might include library suppliers, local and national politicians, other staff in the parent organization and a very wide range of interests in the community of users and potential users.

This simple form of 'market segmentation' is undeniably useful, and is well covered in the literature. However marketing theory has now moved on and it is now recognised that it is no longer enough to discuss what people are, but also to consider what they do and why they do it. A library's publics can therefore be divided according to a number of different factors:
1. *Demographic factors:* This will lead to the consideration of such things as age, sex, class, family size, education, ethnic and religious backgrounds.
2. *Geographic factors:* These require the examination of such things as present and future population patterns and the type of residential area in which people live.
3. On the basis of their behaviour, such as people's use of services and their use and awareness of different communications media.
4. *Psychological factors:* Marketing and PR experts in other fields have developed what they call 'consumer personality scales', identifying the 'thrifty', the 'experimental' and 'traditional' consumer.
5. *Life style:* This leads to the consideration of peoples' activities, interests and opinions.
6. *Benefit segmentation:* This seeks to discover the causes of consumers' and users' behaviour. Not all people seek the same thing from libraries and this approach examines the different 'uses and gratifications' provided by services.[11]

Hopefully, when producing library publicity, such demographic factors as ethnic origin are taken into account and leaflets are produced in the languages of the minority groups in the community. However it is not always clear that enough thought has gone into this type of communication. For instance, it is often assumed that it is enough simply to translate our posters and other publicity. This is not always the case. People's ability to read and cope with language and print varies greatly. Many older Gujaratis, for example, cannot read their own first language. Official, formally worded local government leaflets may become almost incomprehensible when 'translated'. There is for example no Gujarati equivalent of 'meals on wheels' so when translated not only does it have no meaning but it also becomes a source of mild amusement.[12] So to quote a NACAB report, 'Rather than producing a leaflet in English and translating it into other languages, it would be more culturally and linguistically related and subsequently be a more effective medium of transmission if the leaflet was produced accurately in the minority language in the first place.'[13]

The classification of people according to their type of residential area has been found to be an important aid to targeting communications. Indeed in Sheffield we have one free magazine which is only distributed in the more affluent areas of the city; called *West Side* this specialises in publicity for up-market restaurants, real estate, holidays and the like. One may abhor this particular example but no doubt readers will see the relevance of the technique.

People's use of services and their affection for particular forms of media are obviously important factors in helping library managers decide which form of publicity to use. Psychographic segmentation can help practitioners design communication so that it appeals to the experimentalist or the traditionalist or the thrifty consumer. Life style classification does require a considerable amount of research, and the cost may be beyond many library organizations, but to quote the market research manager at Heinz it 'can be useful in fleshing out personality types to whom advertising campaigns, or packaging designs in particular, should be addressed.'[14]

This brings us to what is now called 'benefit segmentation'. A number of years ago I wrote: 'From the point of view of both evaluating and shaping a promotional communication it is important to take . . . audience factors into account'. I went on to say that we must consider 'the audience's motivation — i.e., what does the audience seek from its relationship with a library'. Having discovered that, one is in a better position to design a communication which suggests that the library will appeal to a particular individual or group. McGarry and Burrell have identified six appeals that can be used by library organizations.[15] These and other 'appeals' are identified in *The visible library*.[16]

Commercial advertisements often include a message which has little or nothing to do with the actual product or service being promoted. The nude woman on the car bonnet, the macho male that appears after a Badedas bath not only gain the audience's attention but in addition carry other implications. Thus the car or the bath oil are given an appeal beyond that of transportation or cleanliness.

One hopes that few librarians would wish to use those precise methods. Indeed John Berry, for instance, has written that library promotion should not have 'the same look, sound and tone of all the slick stuff that convinces us we can't shave with one razor blade, or can't succeed if the knees of our pantyhose sag'.[17] It is then necessary to remember the different objectives of organizations that provide a service to make money and organizations that require money to provide a service.

In the space available it has not been possible to examine each of the audience factors in great detail but suffice it to say that the consideration of each of those factors can help make public relations programmes more effective. Benefit segmentation may ultimately prove the most useful but the success or otherwise of a public relations activity does not only depend on the campaign strategy or the communications channel that is used. External factors and the nature of the audience are factors that need also to be considered. When I studied library PR in the USA in the mid seventies I heard of a number of good campaigns that failed in the face of the then popular movement to cut public expenditure and more particularly the property tax. Of course even when a library has been successful in 'reaching' the public with a message, that message has to be interpreted.

There are a number of examples of advertisements having an impact quite different from that intended. The most famous case is probably that of Strand cigarettes. This television advertisement featured a Frank Sinatra-like figure walking alone along a deserted rain swept street. The voice-over stated, "You are never alone with a Strand". It was a fine piece of filmaking, the 'lonely man' became a household name, everybody knew of the advert but hardly anybody bought the cigarette; the reason being that the message taken from the commercial was that Strand smokers had few friends, and as such it was not a product most people wanted to buy or identify with. This example demonstrates that however technically good a campaign, individual psychological, sociological, geographical and other circumstances will cause some people to discount, distrust or simply ignore the message. To quote Hayakawa, 'the meanings of words are not in the words, *they are in us*'.[18]

However this must not stop us from attempting to communicate the value of library and information organizations. The information professions need to acquire a higher social and political profile. As professionals we need to communicate continuously with other information and knowledge workers; we must meet too with our users and potential users in public library communities, in the academic and commercial worlds. Above all we require an effective lobby to communicate positively the value of librarianship, libraries, and information services to politicians, the media and others who can influence public opinion and social policy. Effective public relations activities by information service organizations is then essential at a time when so many other institutions and causes are competing for the public purse and the public's attention.

REFERENCES

1. BERNAYS, E.L. *Crystallising public opinion* New York: Boni and Liveright, 1926.
2. JENKINS, S. Throwing the book at public libraries, *Sunday Times*, 18.10.87.
3. BERGER, P. An investigation of the relationship between public relations activities and budget allocation in public libraries. *Information Processing and Management,* 15(4), 1979, 179-195.
4. JOSEY, E.J. Using grass roots organisation to support library service *Public Libraries,* 22(1), Spring, 1983, 14-16.
5. BLACK, S. *The role of public relations in management.* London: Pitman, 1972.
6. NOVELLI, W.D. Advertising and promotions for public sector and nonprofit services. *In:* Rothschild, M.L. *Marketing communications.* London: D.C. Heath and Co., 1987, 722-723.
7. DOWLIN, K. reported in: Library pioneer looks ahead. *Information World Review,* 2 March 1986, 7.
8. RENBORG, G. Library public relations. *In:* Kent, A. (ed) *Encyclopaedia of Library and Information Science,* Vol. 37, Supplement 2. New York: Marcel Dekker Inc. 1984. 234-265.
9. TOTTERDELL, B. *and* BIRD, J. *The effective library.* (Report of the Hillingdon Project on public library effectiveness). M. Redfern, (ed). London: Library Association, 1976.
10. USHERWOOD, R.C. Public relations is a management tool. *Assistant Librarian,* 76(3), March 1983, 37-42.

11. For a much more detailed review of market segmentation see: Chapter 4 of FRAIN, J. *The principles and practice of marketing*. London: Pitman, 1986, on which this section is based.
12. ACHARYA, D. *Information and advisory provision for Gujaratis in Belgrave area of Leicester*. Study submitted in partial fulfilment of the requirements of Master of Science in Information Studies. (Social Sciences), unpublished dissertation, University of Sheffield, 1987.
13. NATIONAL ASSOCIATION OF CITIZENS' ADVICE BUREAUX. *The Kirklees ethnic minorities advice project — final report. CAB Occasional Paper No. 16* London: NACAB, 1984.
14. HEAD, M. *What do manufacturers want to know about people?* London: ADMAP Publications Ltd., 1981 Quoted in FRAIN, J. *The principles and practice of marketing*. London: Pitman, 1986.
15. McGARRY, K. *and* BURRELL, T.W. *Communication studies — a programmed guide*. London: Bingley, 1973.
16. USHERWOOD, R.C. *The visible library*. London: Library Association, 1981.
17. BERRY, J. The selling of the library. *Library Journal*, 99(2), 16 Jan. 1974, 85.
18. HAYAKAWA, S.I. *Language in thought and action*. 4th ed. New York: Harcourt Brace Jovanovich, 1978.